OI    $3⁰⁰

# Adolph Gottlieb

by **Robert Doty** ASSOCIATE CURATOR
WHITNEY MUSEUM OF AMERICAN ART

and **Diane Waldman** ASSISTANT CURATOR
THE SOLOMON R. GUGGENHEIM MUSEUM

PUBLISHED FOR THE

WHITNEY MUSEUM OF AMERICAN ART AND

THE SOLOMON R. GUGGENHEIM MUSEUM

BY FREDERICK A. PRAEGER, PUBLISHERS

NEW YORK • WASHINGTON • LONDON

*Cover:* original design by Adolph Gottlieb
*Frontispiece:* photograph of the artist by Frank Lloyd
Photographs for this catalogue were made by
Oliver Baker, Geoffrey Clements, Robert Mates, and Paul Katz

Published in the United States of America in 1968
by Frederick A. Praeger, Inc., Publishers
111 Fourth Avenue, New York, N. Y. 10003
77-79 Charlotte Street, London W. 1, England
Library of Congress Catalog Card Number: 68-19542
All rights reserved

Copyright © 1968 by the Whitney Museum of American Art, New York
Designed by Susan Draper Tundisi
Printed in the United States of America
  by Publishers Printing — Admiral Press, New York

# acknowledgements

On behalf of the Whitney Museum of American Art and The Solomon R. Guggenheim Museum, we would like to thank those who have helped to make the exhibition and catalogue possible. They are: Albright-Knox Art Gallery, Buffalo; The Larry Aldrich Museum, Ridgefield, Connecticut; The Art Institute of Chicago; The Joan and Lester Avnet Collection; Mr. Benjamin Baldwin; Mr. Charles B. Benenson; Colonel Samuel A. Berger; Brandeis University Art Collection, Waltham, Massachusetts; Mr. J. Frederic Byers III; Columbia University Art Collection, New York; The Community Synagogue of Sands Point; The Dallas Museum of Fine Arts; Isaac Delgado Museum of Art, New Orleans; Mr. Harold Diamond; Mr. W. Hawkins Ferry; Flint Institute of Arts, Flint, Michigan; Mr. Adolph Gottlieb; Mrs. Adolph Gottlieb; Mr. and Mrs. Boris N. Greenberg; Mr. Clement Greenberg; The Solomon R. Guggenheim Museum, New York; Mr. and Mrs. Ben Heller; The High Museum of Art, Atlanta, Georgia; Mrs. Frederick W. Hilles; Joseph H. Hirshhorn Collection; Mrs. Martha Jackson; Mr. Jack H. Klein; Dr. Morton M. Kligerman; Mr. and Mrs. Samuel M. Kootz; Krannert Art Museum, University of Illinois, Urbana; Dr. and Mrs. Norman Laskey; Mr. George T. Lee, Jr.; Mr. and Mrs. Alexander Lerner; Mr. and Mrs. Albert A. List; The Metropolitan Museum of Art, New York; The Museum of Modern Art, New York; Mr. and Mrs. Roy R. Neuberger; The North Carolina Museum of Art, Raleigh; The Phillips Collection, Washington, D.C.; Mr. and Mrs. Harvey Probber; Mr. and Mrs. Lawrence Richmond; Mr. and Mrs. Bernard Rosenthal; Mr. and Mrs. Robert A. Rowan; Mr. William S. Rubin; Mr. and Mrs. A. I. Sherr; Joseph E. Seagram & Sons, Inc.; Mr. and Mrs. David M. Solinger; The Virginia Museum of Fine Arts, Richmond; Mrs. Samuel Weiner; Walker Art Center, Minneapolis; Mr. and Mr. Barney Weinger; Whitney Museum of American Art, New York; Yale University Art Gallery, New Haven.

Mr. Martin Friedman, Director of the Walker Art Center, Minneapolis, Minnesota, placed all his research on the artist at our disposal. His interviews with Gottlieb have been invaluable in the preparation of the catalogue, and he very graciously discussed his many insights to the artist's work.

In research, we have had generous assistance from Mr. André Emmerich; Mrs. Martha Jackson; Mr. Sidney Janis; Miss Heather Morgan, Marlborough-Gerson Gallery; and Mrs. Annabelle S. Bullen, Whitney Museum of American Art. Much of the original work on the exhibition was based on the artist's exhibition at the Walker Art Center and the catalogue by Mr. Martin Friedman and Miss Suzanne Foley.

Mr. Stephen Weil has served the exhibition constantly, both from the staff of the Marlborough-Gerson Gallery and the staff of the Whitney Museum of American Art. We are grateful for his assistance and enthusiasm. The bibliography has been edited and prepared for the press by Mrs. Patricia FitzGerald Mandel, Research Curator, Whitney Museum of American Art. Miss Gail Korn has assisted both in the exhibition and in preparation of the catalogue.

Mr. Thomas B. Hess; The Museum of Modern Art; Time, Inc.; and the Walker Art Center have lent color plates. The following have provided special assistance in the production of the catalogue: Mr. and Mrs. Lester Avnet, Mr. Charles B. Benenson, Colonel Samuel A. Berger, Mr. and Mrs. Boris N. Greenberg, Mr. Jack H. Klein, Mr. and Mrs. Alexander Lerner, Marlborough-Gerson Gallery, Mr. and Mrs. Roy R. Neuberger, Mr. and Mrs. Harvey Probber, Mr. and Mrs. David M. Solinger.

*Robert Doty and Diane Waldman*

# contents

# part I

*Webster's* defines a pictograph as:

1) an ancient or prehistoric drawing or painting on a rock wall. 2) one of the symbols belonging to a pictorial graphic system. 3) a diagram representing statistical data by pictorial forms varied in color, size, or number to indicate change.

In a statement of 1955, Adolph Gottlieb said: "I adopted the term Pictograph for my paintings out of a feeling of disdain for the accepted notions of what a painting should be. This was in 1941. I decided that to acquiese in the prevailing conception of what constituted 'good painting' meant the acceptance of an academic straitjacket. It was therefore necessary for me to utterly repudiate so-called 'good painting' in order to be free to express what was visually true for me."[1]

For the painters of the New York School, who later became identified as 'Abstract Expressionists', American art of the thirties, whether the routine academicism of the regional scene painters or the neo-plastic dogma of the American Abstract Artists, offered few formal possibilities. Many of this pioneer generation of Abstract Expressionists, Gottlieb among them, had in fact practiced some form of representational painting during the depression years, often under the auspices of the WPA. It was in a spirit of rebellion, not only against the prevailing American art but also against their own early efforts, that they began the search for a new means of expression. The arrival of many of the major European painters shortly before World War II acted as the catalyst. The Surrealists — Max Ernst, Yves Tanguy, André Masson, and the poet laureate of the movement, André Breton — arrived en masse. Duchamp was already active here; Leger and Mondrian lived and worked in New York during the war. They brought with them their enormous vitality and wealth of ideas, and a sense of the entire history of European painting. With the war on, cut off from Europe, it was the surrealists who proved the major influence on the Americans after Cubism. The personal contact with the Surrealists, though limited, provided direct access to their work and reassured the fledgling American painters that the legendary Europeans were, after all, human, not gods. Arshile Gorky, Jackson Pollock, Willem de Kooning, Robert Motherwell, Mark Rothko and Adolph Gottlieb were among the earliest admirers of this new art from Europe. For all of them, it was an exhilarating time, a moment in history that gave them the freedom and the challenge they needed to cut the umbilical ties to a provincial American art. From this alliance with European art and thought they created, with one monumental effort, a brilliant new American art.

It was against this background that Gottlieb was able to break away from the limitations of his earlier painting and to develop his mature style which began with the Pictographs. The Pictographs which date, in the strictest sense, from 1941-1951, form one of the two major phases of Gottliem's career to date, of which the most recent is the series known as the Bursts. Between the Pictographs and the Bursts, which date from 1957 to the present, are two subsidiary themes, the Grids and the Imaginary Landscapes, each of which occurs in tangential relationship to the two major periods. Together they form an impressive body of work spanning nearly thirty years, and document the gradual but consistent evolution of his style.

Adolph Gottlieb was born in New York City on March 14, 1903. He left high school in 1920 to work at various part-time jobs. At night he studied at the Art Students League with John Sloan and attended the lectures of Robert Henri. Sloan was interested in what was happening in France, particularly in the structural ideas of Cubism; he also admired Cézanne, Van Gogh and the other Post Impressionists. It was from these two traditional painters that Gottlieb formed his first awareness of the revolutionary break-throughs in early twentieth century European painting. In 1921, Gottlieb heard of a job on a ship and, on the spur of the moment, packed a bag and went off to Europe. He stayed in Paris for six months, attending sketch classes at the Académie de la Grande Chaumière and did some drawing and painting. He went to the Louvre constantly and to the galleries. Always rather aloof, he frequented the Sylvia Beach bookshop encountering other American and European artists and writers but making few friends and meeting none of the French artists whose work he had been introduced to at the Art

**Sundeck.** 1936.
Oil on canvas. 24 x 36.
Courtesy of the University of Maryland.

**Still Life — Dry Cactus.** c. 1938.
Oil on canvas. 36 x 48.
Courtesy of the artist.

**The Sea Chest.** 1942.
Oil on canvas. 26 x 34.
The Solomon R. Guggenheim Museum.


Students League. Gottlieb spent the next year traveling around Europe, to Berlin
and Munich, with brief visits to the Museums in Vienna, Dresden, and Prague.
When he returned to the United States in 1923, he finished high school and entered
the Parsons School of Design to prepare for teaching. He then decided against
teaching and supported himself on part-time jobs while painting full-time. In 1929,
he entered the Dudensing National Competition, an annual event sponsored by
the Dudensing Gallery in New York and juried by prominent critics. Gottlieb won a
first prize, shared with Konrad Cramer, for a group of vaguely 'expressionistic'
figures and landscapes. The prize for the competition, an exhibition at the
Dudensing Gallery, took place the following May, to generally favorable reviews
but no sales. The gallery closed shortly after. By the mid-thirties, Gottlieb was
exhibiting regularly with a New York avant-garde group known as The Ten, among
whom were Ilya Bolotowsky, Mark Rothko and Lee Gatch. The group, who were
mutually sympathetic to each other's work, somehow never numbered more
than nine and were commonly referred to as "The Ten who are Nine."[2]

The Dudensing award was useful in getting Gottlieb a place on the Federal Art
Project in 1936 as an easel painter. The only requirement of the program was a
periodic distribution of an artist's production to public institutions, primarily
hospitals and schools; there was never any interference with the way in which he
was working. His paintings were generally landscapes painted indoors from
sketches made out-of-doors at Gloucester, Massachusetts, during the summer

of that year. In 1937, he left the WPA and moved to a small community outside Tucson, Arizona with his wife Esther. He did more work that year than he had at any prior time. In Arizona his subject matter changed; he picked up pieces of dried cactus and gourds in the desert and created a series of still-lifes with them by arranging these slightly modeled objects on a table top tipped forward parallel to the picture plane. He has said that some of the ovoid desert shapes still carry through, "... in the disc forms I use now ...",[3] and it is tempting to visualize the Bursts in his recollections of the Arizona landscape where the vast expanse of sky made it possible to see the horizon for 360 degrees.

The feeling of isolation prompted his return to New York in 1939; from there he went to Gloucester where he began a series of beach still-lifes, arranging seashells, starfish, and coral in three dimensional boxes set against deeply receding, ultimately irrational spaces, like the *Sea Chest* of 1942, a later but related painting. He soon abandoned this form of 'Magic Realism' (derived from Salvador Dali) for the Pictographs but the relationship between them is quite apparent. The earlier compartments were replaced by recilinear subdivisions, the complete object by its symbolic counterpart, the surreal space by the flat two dimensional surface of the canvas. In the *Sea Chest,* the thoughtful adjustment of shapes — the juxtaposition of a smooth rounded seashell with a sharp jagged one, and the play of their curves against the vertical-horizontal structure of the chest — becomes one of the most insistent pictorial devices of his paintings, achieving even greater significance in the Pictographs and culminating with the Bursts. These seascapes of 1939-1940 became the means by which Gottlieb could effect the transition from the earliest 'academic' figure, landscape, and still-life paintings of the thirties to the Pictographs of the forties.

The first Pictograph, *The Eyes of Oedipus,* of 1941, is a somewhat tentative exploration of the possibilities inherent in the use of a pictographic imagery. Nevertheless, it establishes the essential framework for the Pictographs in the creation of a dialectical tension between line and symbol-as-form. To secure the desired equilibrium, Gottlieb sacrificed color in the early Pictographs for virtually monochromatic effects. In the use of half tones and close values, in the radical flattening of space and form, and, indeed, in several of the images themselves, the paintings reflect an adaptation of the Cubist esthetic. There may also be something of an awareness of Mondrian in the surface divisions of the canvas, especially in a pictograph like *The Eyes of Oedipus,* but Gottlieb by no means shares Mondrian's impassioned regard for the stringencies of the plus-minus system. What Gottlieb does establish, by means of his linear organization, is a certain affinity to Mondrian in terms of an all-over image and an awareness of both the edge of the canvas and its surface plane. The division of the pictographic surface suggests that he arrived at this stage by virtue of his own compartmented still-lifes of 1939-1940; its random pattern is an adaptation of the automatism practised by the Surrealists. Starting with the grid, whose form he arrived at intuitively, Gottlieb would select a shape, for example an eye, at random, and place it in one of the compartments. Without any predetermination, he would add image after image until he was satisfied that a painting had achieved its final form. References to a hand, a face, an eye, teeth or other parts of the human anatomy are the residual data of his earlier interest in the figure; in the Pictographs the members are isolated to enhance their emotive powers. They are part of a repertory of image-symbols (others include snakes, birds, masks, eggs) that he discovered in past art forms which appeared to him to have a universal significance, or in Jungian terms, to form part of a "collective unconscious." Removed from their original culture, however, they lose the context, the connective tissue, which is crucial to their original meaning and use; they become, instead, virtually abstract signs without significant mythic content. It is interesting to speculate that the introduction of primitive forms at this time was required (like Dubuffet's) primarily for pictorial reasons (automatism) rather than for the interest in myth as such; certainly, its use was widespread among the New York School, the most noted among them Gorky, Pollock, Baziotes, Gottlieb and Rothko. Gottlieb and Rothko worked closely together in the early 1940's to develop the idea of myth in their paintings. In a statement to *The New York Times* of June 13, 1943, clarifying their esthetic beliefs, Gottlieb and Rothko stated their interest in myth:

1. To us art is an adventure into an unknown world, which can be explored only by those willing to take the risks.

2. This world of the imagination is fancy-free and violently opposed to common sense.

3. It is our function as artists to make the spectator see our way, not his way.

4. We favor the simple expression of the complex thought. We are for the large shape because it has the impact of the unequivocal. We wish to reassert the picture plane. We are for flat forms because they destroy illusion and reveal truth.

5. It is a widely accepted notion among painters that it does not matter what one paints as long as it is well painted. This is the essence of academism. There is no such thing as good painting about nothing. We assert that the subject is crucial and only that subject-matter is valid which is tragic and timeless. That is why we profess spiritual kinship with primitive and archaic art.[4]

The use of myth, whether Northwest Coast Indian, African or Freudian, offered Gottlieb a way of forcibly breaking with American tradition; of even more importance was its stimulation of a new and vital vocabulary of images. The Pictographs have been variously identified with Surrealism, primitive art, American Indian petroglyphs, 14th century Italian predella panels, and with totems, psychoanalysis, and private symbolism. Although the vocabulary of signs that Gottlieb developed over the years often brings with it references to another order, it is always part of a larger pictorial vision and in this sense the symbols have little relationship to their original sources. That the use of myth served as a timely subject matter is suggested by the fact that both Gottlieb and Rothko abandoned mythical signs for a virtually abstract imagery a few years later.

Once chrystallized, the grid provided Gottlieb with a fecund working formula for the next fifteen years. It offered him several alternatives: forms could either be neatly compartmented within any or all of the rectangles shaped by the intersecting verticals and horizontals of the grid (as in *Pictograph,* 1942, *Evil Omen,* 1946, *Bent Arrow,* 1949, *Male and Female,* 1950), they can spill out over the structure (*Alkahest of Paracelsus,* 1945, *Recurrent Apparition,* 1946, *Hidden Image,* 1950), or they can

**Romanesque Facade.** 1949.
Oil on canvas. 48 x 36.
Lent by the Krannert Art Museum,
University of Illinois.

imply a tacit awareness of the grid without its actual use (*Dream,* 1948, *Figuration of Clangor,* 1951, *Composition,* 1955). Or he could subvert it by other means: with wedges of color underlying or placed over the grid, by blurring the contour between two forms, by the use of a dense impasto blanketing the surface of the canvas, and by filling only certain compartments with images. The size and placement of the forms set up a rhythmic progression whose directional force is in opposition to the static nature of the grid.

The earliest pictographs, those dating from 1941-46, are generally more linear than the later ones, the paint more thinly applied. Gottlieb often used a mixture of oil and egg tempera which enabled him to paint thinly and to overlay certain areas with opaque white lines. In the *Alkahest of Paracelsus* and related paintings of the mid-forties, rich greens, browns and blacks predominate. The look is that of weathered bark or wood, like the tribal masks and sculpture he started collecting in 1935. Primitive forms are common to the paintings of the mid-forties; they mingle with biomorphic and scatalogical forms adapted from Arp, Miro, Masson. They are part of a vocabulary of subject matter which attained, in the late forties and early fifties, a stability and sophistication by a process of elimination, repetition and refinement.

In 1947 and 1948, but more particularly in 1949, 1950, 1951, a looser, more brushed surface gradually asserts its priority over the grid and the images. Color, too, becomes softer, fuller, more modulated, and eventually more brilliant. Color and form disturb the static sense of the surface and the total ambience becomes one of easy fluctuation. The paintings reveal a love of pigment that in its sensuous expansion is reminiscent of Impressionism. The period of the early fifties is characterized by still another adjustment between the painterly and the linear: the grids re-emerge as thick black lines in an erratic, less vertical-horizontal arrangement. The vigorous all-over pattern has certain affinities to the webs of Pollock although the intent is entirely different, for Gottlieb, even in a painting of the size of *Labyrinth,* of 1954, never loses the sense of scale of easel painting. Gottlieb achieves some wonderful effects with this group, to which he gave the title of Grids. The contrast between the tracery of black lines and one or two colors juxtaposed in shallow layers creates a soft luminosity and a perceptible, if ambiguous, depth. It was an idea that he had attempted earlier, in the *Sounds at Night,* of 1948, for example, but it reaches its most successful expression in paintings like *Labyrinth* or *Blue at Noon,* 1955.[5]

Two parts to Gottlieb slowly emerge: the constant reference to illusion — the unwillingness to allow a canvas to remain flat — by overlapping paint of different colors, by transparencies or translucencies, by line on top of a plane, by multiple superimposed lines, by paint spilling over lines. One is left with veils of paint of differing depths, in different parts of the canvas. The veils also make reference to time sequences, in which forms are located in space in front of (or behind) other objects. Time also becomes readable in a literal sense with regard to the physical devotion Gottlieb lavished on certain areas of the canvas. Often, the paintings are reminiscent of a carpet of grass with small and fragmented meticulously planted flowers.

/ 16

It is at this point, within the area of a reconnaissance of symbols, of an aerial observation by a painterly hand, that the work became not broad enough, as in *Labyrinth,* nor calligraphic enough, as in *T,* of 1950, and started to move towards an object, as in *Unstill Life,* 1952, and *Unstill Life III,* 1954-56. With *Unstill Life* of 1952, the contraction away from the outside edges of the canvas, and the establishment of a ground (whether this was first or last is irrelevant) created the perimeter of his invented object, the Burst. Yet, both of the Unstill Lifes retain their affinities to the earlier work. Once this aspect of his development was secured, Gottlieb began to float two or three simple shapes, forms that had previously existed in the total Pictograph structure, around his invented object. For this group of works, the Imaginary Landscapes, Gottlieb again delved into his own paintings for these shapes, and in *Man and Arrow* of 1950, he begins to articulate the relationship between his invented object and a secondary object, one devoid of symbolic intent other than color, that is fulfilled in the Bursts.

DIANE WALDMAN

[1] Adolph Gottlieb: Statement for the 1955 Annual Exhibition of Contemporary American Painting, University of Illinois, November 9, 1955-January 8, 1956. The statement was not published in the catalogue.

[2] Other regulars included Louis Schanker, Ben-Zion, Earl Kerkam, Joseph Solman, Louis Harris.

[3] Adolph Gottlieb: taped interview with Martin Friedman, 1962.

[4] The statement, which was drafted by Gottlieb and Rothko with the aid of Barnett Newman, was a rebuttal to the critic of The New York Times, Edward Alden Jewell, who accused Gottlieb and Rothko of fostering a new movement that he called Globalism. This attack first appeared in The New York Times of June 6, 1943.

[5] For an accurate discussion of Gottlieb's influence on Bradley Walker Tomlin see: John I. H. Baur, *Bradley Walker Tomlin,* Whitney Museum of American Art, 1957, pp 26-29.

**Burst.** 1957.
Oil on canvas. 96 x 40.
Lent by Mr. and Mrs. Ben Heller.

**part II**   "I think you have to keep in mind that my painting has always been conceptual . . . there always is a framework which is a purely arbitrary thing."[1] A clearly conceived arrangement of elements has formed the core of Adolph Gottlieb's painting, from the first mature works to the present day. He has always sought, and found, some pictorial or iconographical system upon which to structure his images. He has spoken of "a schematic arrangement," "some notion of style," "the process of making a painting," indicating his programatic approach to the problems of putting paint to canvas. For years artists have relied on formal systems such as contrasts of light and dark or vanishing-point perspective. Gottlieb, in the contemporary tradition, has invented pictorial systems to suit his own needs and intentions. The Pictographs are built upon the grid-shape arrangement of horizontal and vertical lines, the Imaginary Landscapes are predicated on the use of a horizontal line to divide the canvas, and the Bursts utilize two or more shapes opposed on a vertical axis. Such carefully ordered foundations are basic to a man who believes "The act of painting must be rational, objective and consciously disciplined."[2]

Objectivity has never been the only source of Gottlieb's strength. His rationality has consistently been tempered by an intuitive awareness of the significant gesture, the perceptive touch. The approach to the canvas was pre-planned, but the action on its surface was a unique and unanticipated experience. He became as much involved with the flow of creating as the ordering of his concepts. The choice of a color, the direction of a line, the acceptance of chance in laying paint, result from impulsive decisions. The process of painting had become entwined with personal revelation. William Baziotes recalled "What happens on the canvas is unpredictable and surprising to me,"[3] and Jackson Pollock said, "When I am in my painting, I'm not aware of what I'm doing."[4] Gottlieb, too, was involved with the lure of the subconscious. The Pictographs, "stem from introspection, free association and automatism," and he told Selden Rodman, "Painting is self-discovery. You arrive at the image through the act of painting."[5] During the past fifteen years the act has assumed primacy as the conceptual structure was reduced to a minimum.

Over the years, Gottlieb's painting has become monumental. As his concepts developed, they simplified. The culmination of Gottlieb's schematic arrangement was reached in the painting *Burst*. It was immediately hailed as a milestone by the critic Clement Greenberg: "What makes such a picture difficult — difficult in the best sense — is its monumental simplicity, which seems more than the conventions of easel painting can tolerate."[6] In their manifesto of 1943, Adolph Gottlieb and

Mark Rothko stated, "We favor the simple expression of the complex thought,"[7] and Gottlieb has steadily adhered to that maxim. "I always felt it was necessary to give up a lot of things as I went along,"[8] he said recently. The multiple symbols and the lattice-like structure of the Pictographs were discarded for the horizon line and illusory space of the Imaginary Landscapes. The rigid format of the Landscapes dissolved into the fluid space of the Bursts. Through reduction and simplification he has achieved a canvas which evokes a sense of the absolute and opens the way to a confrontation with color and surface, for reduction did not include absolute purification. The most recent paintings are distinguished by lavish color and gestural effects, but they rely essentially on a basic simplicity.

Reliance on pictorial systems and conventions establishes a unity within Gottlieb's work. Repetitive imagery and iconography have brought about a continuity that flows from the Pictographs to the most recent paintings. Retention of familiar themes and devices was vital to his highly disciplined, carefully considered manner of working. It has been a process of refinement, constantly improving, constantly seeking perfection in every aspect. Self-imposed limitation of means permitted greater freedom to examine the content of his art. By methodically choosing to limit the area he could explore, he has been able to analyze and exploit the sensual, expressive gist of color, shape, and line in myriad variations.

The Abstract Expressionists maintained a scrupulous regard for the integrity of the picture plane. In 1943, Gottlieb and Rothko spoke of their wish to "reassert the picture plane," and three years later Gottlieb described the grid of the Pictograph as "a device to kill space," by which he meant the illusion traditionally created by means of vanishing-point perspective. Space was denied in the Pictograph by placing the grid and the symbols on the surface and carrying the lines of the grid to the edges of the canvas. In the Imaginary Landscapes, the suggestion of space was allowed to re-appear. But it was a sense of space limited by the horizontal line and the location of shapes and lines on the same frontal, vertical plane. This taut handling of spatial relations was intensified in the Bursts by retaining the placement of forms on the single, vertical axis and eliminating all reference to the edge of the canvas. Shapes and lines are hung on the picture plane, suspended over the background. This has been Gottlieb's essential procedure for structuring the paintings during the past decade. His attention to the picture plane is a basic tenet. "I'm preoccupied with maintaining a certain plane that goes right across the surface of the canvas, regardless of the methods that I use. This is one of the problems . . . if I use a jet black jagged form or a calligraphic big, thick line which streaks across the bottom of the canvas, how to keep this related to the rectangle, keep it on the surface and maintain this integrity of the surface."[9]

Looking back upon the formative years of Abstract Expressionism, Robert Motherwell listed the new concerns of the painter: "Pictures were mat, flat, the picture plane was respected, etc. What was crucial (and how!) was the development of the large format."[10] Clement Greenberg has suggested that Arshile Gorky led the way with big pictures in the early 1940's. He was soon followed by Jackson Pollock, who expanded the size of the canvas to accommodate his whole body in the act of painting. The immediate precedent for big pictures were the murals in public buildings which many Abstract Expressionists, including Gottlieb, had worked on during the 1930's. He returned to architectural projects in 1951, and again in 1952, when he was commissioned to design tapestries for two synagogues.

These were followed, in 1952, by a major project. He was asked to design the 1,300-square-foot glass facade for the Milton Steinberg Memorial Center in New York. Treating the space as a vast whole, he created a series of related compartments containing linear designs. He followed this work on a grand scale by increasing the size of his canvases and by 1957 had produced, among others, two that were sixteen feet long each, a limit imposed by the dimension of his studio. The new sense of scale was an expedient which perfectly suited his temperament, and after the introduction of the Bursts he frequently worked on large paintings. He never begins a large canvas with preparatory drawing, and his willingness to let experience guide his progress induces a feeling of spontaneity which tends to prevent stasis, a danger in a large work. Like Mark Rothko, Clyfford Still, and Barnett Newman, who present in their paintings a monolithic impression of color, he expects to have the painting seen and felt as an entity, a single image. The immediate impact is all-important. Once engaged by the presence of the work, the spectator is free to enjoy its rich components.

Gottlieb is a colorist. He early admired the soft color used by Milton Avery and introduced rather flamboyant, pastel-like shades in the late Pictographs. From those brilliant hues, through the subdued tones of the early Bursts and Landscapes, to the lush complexity of the recent work, he has perfected as fine a cognizance for the value of color as any painter of his time. Such paintings as *Black Black, Equal,* and *Focal* are enriched by colors of a complexity rarely seen in modern painting. Various critics have remarked upon his singular ability to handle color and Clement Greenberg regarded it as Gottlieb's finest characteristic. Control of the image has been present throughout his career, but the color sense has been gradually improving over the years, with the result that linear structure has taken a subordinate role to the interaction of color areas and the relationships of colors within those areas. "I want to express the utmost intensity of the color, bring out the quality, make it expressive. At the same time, I would also like to bring out a certain immaterial character that it can have, so that it exists as sensation and a feeling that it will carry nuances not necessarily inherent in the color, which are brought out by juxtaposition."[11] His use of color is subject to the rational, disciplined approach that is the foundation for all his work. He is well aware of the tremendous range of value in color and uses it to full advantage. Whether light or dark hues, his colors always contain a high degree of luminosity, especially in the later works, where, favoring such tints as pink, green, yellow, his grounds give the effect of brilliant illumination. The free forms of the Imaginary Landscapes are treated with flat primary colors, the intensity of blue, red, yellow balancing the solidarity of black, while a great range of color variants fill the ground of the Bursts to the point of saturation. But at a certain point intuition becomes operative as well, and the choice of a certain color may be dictated by impulse. This is the point at which feeling takes over from rationality. "I use color in terms of emotional quality, as a vehicle for feeling...feeling is everything I have experienced or thought."[12] For Gottlieb, color is no longer simply an element of design, it is an agent of expression.

The surface of Gottlieb's paintings is also a highly expressive element in his work. The edge of an area of thick paint, applied with a palette knife, is sometimes worked with a rag and turpentine to achieve a transparent effect and the subsequent contrast between the opaque impasto and the translucent stain. The paint of a disc is treated like a glaze with a resultant increase in light reflection. Heavy, thick paint is sometimes attacked vigorously with the knife so that some splashes outward. Gottlieb accepts spatter technique for its feeling of inherent spontaneity. It is here that the act of painting, the physical force of the hand and arm, is most readily apparent. Gottlieb is not an "action" painter. But he evinces the pleasure of manipulating paint, enjoying the viscous nature of the pigment, or he may scumble, spreading paint as a thin translucent layer. Generally, strong textures have given way to a burnished surface treatment. The sensuous quality of paint serves to emphasize the expressive intent of color. The immediate sensation is a tactile one, an overture to primary reaction and a lure for emotions to be aroused by the visual experience.

From 1950 to 1957, Gottlieb developed new themes, new images. This was a period of gestation, of divesting himself from the need to think about mythology and primordial history in order to concentrate on the painting as a self-sufficient object of visual interest. Stripping a Pictograph of its symbols left the linear struc- ture, or "grid" exposed, so it became the subject. The Grid paintings presented a frenzied jumble of line and space. Their semblance of chaos was a marked contrast to the order of the Pictographs, but the heritage of the latter was still apparent. The inevitable break came as "I started making a Grid, then I decided I didn't want it and I divided the painting into two parts. I wanted a disparate image."[13] He laid a white ground across the writhing, interwoven lines of a grid and on the white ground he laid five areas of flat color in varying shapes. He titled this painting *The Frozen Sounds, Number 1,* the first of a series to be known as Imaginary Landscapes. The division of the canvas suggested a horizon, land and sky, and he accepted that association. But his interest was centered on the formal problems of the format. Especially, he was concerned with the relationship between the forms floating in space and the density of the mass below. The lower area is generally composed with a very fluid brushwork and a network of irregular lines, rich and dense, while the upper ground tends to be an opaque white, con- sistent overall, upon which is superimposed circles, ovals, rectangles or other irregularly geometric shapes. The variations of this theme occupied him intensely until 1957, and exhibitions devoted to the Imaginary Landscapes were held at the Kootz Gallery in 1953, and at the Martha Jackson Gallery in 1957. Gottlieb has continually worked with the landscape format, eventually refining it to the barest essentials. Paintings such as *Dialogue Number 1,* 1960, and *Rolling,* 1961, retain the format of circular shapes in flat, primary colors above the agitated mass of inter- woven black lines. Hence, both shapes and lines are suspended over a common ground, implying infinite space. But in 1965, he returned to the idea of a rectangle composed as two areas, ground and sky. *Units II* and *Units III* re-instate the edge as a boundary, establish explicit areas and introduce a multiplicity of units. The process of making a painting has consistently brought Gottlieb back to the landscape format, to the universal experience of earth and sky, the tension between space and mass.

The work which inaugurated Gottlieb's third major concept was painted in 1957. *Burst* was first shown during Gottlieb's exhibition at The Jewish Museum, New York, in that year. The image was reduced to two forms on a white ground, with no reference to the edge of the rectangle. The colors, black, red, white, are muted and imbued with tonal contrasts. The crucial relation, however, is the disparity between the clearly delinated disc and the ragged outline of the lower form. This black mass retains the earth orientation effect of the lower area in the land- scapes, but the center has become solidified, as though to defy the penetration of light. The disc, however, acts as a light reflector. The inherent attraction of the disc as a motif-sign is the round shape and the contrast between the character of that shape and the inflexibly rectangular format of the picture support. The disc is a potent symbol, and, with the addition of a concentric band, connotes a solid body emanating light rays. Such a device appears in the Pictographs and re-appears frequently in the experimental paintings of the early 1950s. Through the process of reduction and with the introduction of large scale, Gottlieb realized the expressive potential of the disc as a form and it became the most prevalent item in his iconography. He has, of course, worked countless variations in the problem of relating the disc and diverse shapes, at first relying principally upon variations in the outline, number, and size of the shapes. His exhibtion at the Sidney Janis Gallery in 1960, revealed that color had become the means for unifi-

**Equal.** 1964.
Oil on canvas. 20 x 16.
Lent by Mr. Jack H. Klein.

/ 23

cation. The primacy of color permitted further reduction in formal content so that by 1963, the disc was adrift on a field of vivid color, balanced only by a series of short vertical bars of primary color. In works such as *Icon* and *Focal,* the Burst series reaches a climax. The process of reduction has led Gottlieb to a monumentality only rarely achieved in American painting.

In 1961, H. Harvard Arnason surveyed Abstract Expressionist painting and added the classification of "imagist." Concerning Gottlieb, he wrote: "the image begins to develop many different individual associations — landscape, outer space, symbol of order and chaos — whatever the spectator brings to it. While still a completely abstract work, the implication of subject or symbolic content is so strong that it is impossible to think of the picture as essentially an arrangement of abstract color shapes on a two-dimensional surface. The painting is an abstract image."[14] The fact that the sources of his imagery are to be found in nature reinforces the desire of the spectator to associate. The arrangement of space and line in the Imaginary Landscapes compels the spectator to equate the paintings with a natural experience. Indeed, the Imaginary Landscapes often verge on the picturesque. The critic Belle Krasne was moved to describe one as "a chaotic and heaving swamp." The shape of the Burst series is often identified as a "sun," but the ambiguity of space in that series is unrelated to reality. Interpretations of the Bursts have dealt primarily with the ambiguous relation between the forms. Martin Friedman has seen them as "grand images of dualism." Lawrence Alloway has described the forms as "terrestial" and "solar." Gottlieb himself speaks of "polarities." He has also said that "life is a mixture of brutality and beauty," and he noticed in the work of Arshile Gorky "a curious emotional undertone of gentleness and brutality."

For all his thoughts about brutality, it is difficult to find any such manifestation in his work. What does occur, however, is a sense of motion, sometimes steady and resolute, sometimes violent and erratic. The highly charged, energetic quality of his line, the transitory, random aspect of the paint allowed to spatter upon the canvas, and the shapes with no visible means of support, all suggest forces in motion. The titles of his paintings, *Burst, Rolling, Side Pull, Ping, Expanding, Rising,* reinforce the visual impression. Whereas those painters who deliberately based their imagery on the act of painting, and the motion thus invoked, achieved a sense of pictorial balance, Gottlieb, proceeding from a position of deliberation, portrayed action itself. His reflection of the common experience, as translated to canvas, was one of constant flux.

Gottlieb has always been true to his intentions. He has made no claims for the affinitive aspect of his work, and has on several occasions denied such tendencies. "I never use nature as a starting point, I never abstract from nature, I never consciously think of nature when I paint."[15] Thus he repudiates the literal interpretation of the horizontal division of his picture space as a true horizon or the identification of the disc as a sun. "When I work, I'm thinking in terms of purely visual effects and relations; and any verbal equivalent is something that comes afterwards. But it's inconceivable to me that I could experience things and not have them enter into my painting."[16] Rational association holds no interest for him. His goal is the expression of the complex relation of human values and emotions that make up the human spirit.

It has been the role of the expressionist painter to look within himself, to adopt a subjective attitude which in the course of his encounter with the canvas, will become a perception to be shared by everyone. In 1916, Arthur G. Dove wrote: "I should like to enjoy life by choosing all its highest instances, to give back in my means of expression all that it gives to me: to give in form and color the reaction that plastic objects and sensations of light from within and without have reflected from my inner consciousness. Theories have been outgrown, the means is disappearing, the reality of the sensation alone remaining."[17] Both Dove and Gottlieb maintained contact with nature, having spent a major portion of their lives by and on the sea, and both were guided in their image-making by subjective feelings. But Dove was limited to recording impressions of the real world. His reference was to nature and the substance of life, his imagery was a revelation of sensations and impressions. The expressionist painter maintains the process of relating art to experience, but turns inward with increasing concern for self-discovery. Freed of the desire or need to communicate in traditional terms, the Abstract Expressionist painter reveals a world of highly personal reflections. Gottlieb accepted the isolation of the artist in favor of subliminal expression, and, once unhindered by the dominance of nature, has embraced the psychological manifestations of color and form. His paintings of the 1960's have become equivalents of inner forces rather than pictures of experience or ideas. In them are embodied the resolution, knowledge, and ardor that have sustained Gottlieb during a lifetime as a painter.

ROBERT DOTY

[1] Adolph Gottlieb: taped interview with Martin Friedman, 1962.

[2] In *The New Decade: 35 American Painters and Sculptors,* ed., John I. H. Baur, Whitney Museum of American Art, 1955, p 36.

[3] In *William Baziotes,* by Lawrence Alloway, The Solomon R. Guggenheim Museum, 1965, p 16.

[4] In *Jackson Pollock,* by Francis V. O'Connor, The Museum of Modern Art, 1967, p 40.

[5] Selden Rodman: *Conversation with Artists,* Devin-Adair, 1957, p 91.

[6] Clement Greenberg: *An Exhibition of Oil Paintings by Adolph Gottlieb,* The Jewish Museum, 1957, p 7.

[7] Adolph Gottlieb and Mark Rothko: In "The Realm of Art: A New Platform. 'Globalism' Pops Into View," by Edward Alden Jewell, *New York Times,* June 13, 1943.

[8] Conversation with the author, 1967.

[9] Adolph Gottlieb: taped interview with Martin Friedman, 1962.

[10] Robert Motherwell: interview with Max Kozloff, *Art Forum,* 4:1:37 S 1965.

[11] Adolph Gottlieb: taped interview with Martin Friedman, 1962.

[12] Ibid.

[13] Conversation with the author, 1967.

[14] H. Harvard Arnason, *American Abstract Expressionists and Imagists,* The Solomon R. Guggenheim Museum, 1961, p 27.

[15] Adolph Gottlieb: letter to John I. H. Baur, then Associate Director, Whitney Museum of American Art, June 20, 1957.

[16] Adolph Gottlieb: taped interview with Martin Friedman, 1962.

[17] Arthur G. Dove: in *The Forum Exhibition of Modern American Painters,* Mitchell Kennerley, 1916, no page.

plates

**Eyes of Oedipus.** 1941.
Oil on canvas. 32 x 25.
Lent by Mrs. Adolph Gottlieb.

**Pictograph.** 1942.
Oil on canvas. 48 x 36.
Lent by the artist.

**The Red Bird.** 1944.
Oil on canvas. 40 x 30.
The Solomon R. Guggenheim Museum.

**Expectation of Evil.** 1945.
Oil on canvas. 43 x 27.
Lent by the artist.

**The Alkahest of Paracelsus.** 1945.
Oil on canvas. 60 x 44.
Lent by the artist.

**Pictogenic Fragments.** 1946.
Oil on canvas. 36 x 30.
Lent by the Joseph H. Hirshhorn Collection.

**Pendant Image.** 1946.
Oil on canvas. 25 x 32.
The Solomon R. Guggenheim Museum.

**Black Enigma.** 1946.
Oil on canvas. 28 x 34.
Lent by Mr. and Mrs. Lawrence Richmond.

**Evil Omen.** 1946.
Oil on canvas. 38 x 30.
Lent by Mr. and Mrs. Roy R. Neuberger.

**Recurrent Apparition.** 1946.
Oil on canvas. 36 x 54.
Lent by the artist.

**Pictograph.** 1946.
Oil on canvas. 36 x 48.
Lent by Mrs. Martha Jackson.

**Pursuer and Pursued.** 1947.
Oil on canvas. 38 x 36.
Lent by Yale University Art Gallery.
  Gift of Fred Olsen.

**Oracle.** 1947.
Oil on canvas. 60 x 44.
Lent by Mr. and Mrs. Albert A. List.

**Sorceress.** 1947.
Oil on canvas. 48 x 36.
Lent by Columbia University.
   Gift of Mr. and Mrs. Samuel M. Kootz.

**Altar.** 1947.
Oil on canvas. 48 x 36.
Lent by Mr. and Mrs. Samuel M. Kootz.

**Sounds at Night.** 1948.
Oil on canvas. 48 x 60.
Lent by the artist.

**Dream.** 1948.
Oil on canvas. 20 x 24.
Lent by the Isaac Delgado Museum of Art.
  Gift of William March Campbell.

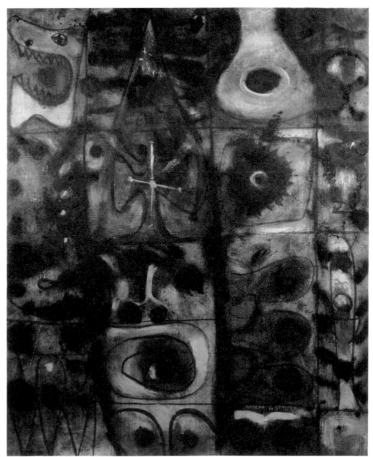

**Water, Air, Fire.** 1947.
Oil on pressed board. 30 x 24.
Lent by Brandeis University Art Collection.
  Gift of Mr. and Mrs. Samuel M. Kootz.

**Sorcerer.** 1948.
Oil on canvas. 38 x 30.
Lent by Mr. Harold Diamond.

**Vigil.** 1948.
Oil on canvas. 36 x 48.
Lent by the Whitney Museum of American Art.

**Man Looking at Woman.** 1949.
Oil on canvas. 42 x 54.
Lent by Mr. William S. Rubin.

**Bent Arrow.** 1949.
Oil on canvas. 36 x 48.
Lent by Mr. and Mrs. Boris N. Greenberg.

**Man and Arrow II.** 1950.
Oil on canvas. 38 x 30.
Lent by Mrs. Adolph Gottlieb.

**Ebb Tide.** 1951.
Oil on canvas. 24 x 30.
Private collection.

**Hidden Image.** 1950.
Oil on canvas. 42 x 54.
Lent by the artist.

**T.** 1950.
Oil on canvas. 48 x 36.
Lent by The Metropolitan Museum of Art.
    David M. and Hope G. Solinger Foundation, Inc.,
    Gift Fund, 1952.

**Male and Female.** 1950.
Oil on burlap. 48 x 60.
Lent by the artist.

**The Seer.** 1950.
Oil on canvas. 60 x 72.
Lent by The Phillips Collection.

**Archer.** 1951.
Oil on canvas. 72 x 60.
Lent by the artist.

**Symbols and a Woman.** 1951.
Oil on canvas. 60 x 72.
Lent by the artist.

**Untitled.** 1951.
Oil on canvas. 48 x 60.
Lent by Mr. and Mrs. Harvey Probber.

**Sentinel.** 1951.
Oil on canvas. 60 x 48.
Lent by the artist.

**Figuration of Clangor.** 1951.
Oil on canvas. 48 x 60.
Lent by the artist.

**Figure.** 1951.
Oil on canvas. 24 x 20.
Lent by Mr. and Mrs. David M. Solinger.

**Tournament.** 1951.
Oil on canvas. 60 x 72.
Lent by Mrs. Adolph Gottlieb.

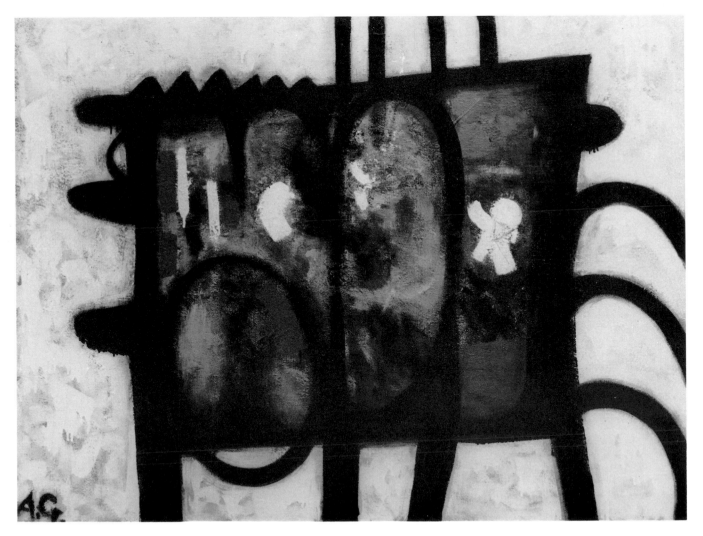

**Unstill Life.** 1952.
Oil on canvas. 36 x 48.
Lent by the Whitney Museum of American Art.
    Gift of Mr. and Mrs. Alfred Jaretzki, Jr.

**Trajectory.** 1954.
Oil on canvas. 40 x 50.
Lent by Mr. and Mrs. Robert A. Rowan.

**Labyrinth III.** 1954.
Oil on canvas. 84 x 192.
Lent by the artist.

**Blue at Noon.** 1955.
Oil on canvas. 60 x 72.
Lent by the Walker Art Center.

**Composition.** 1955.
Oil on canvas. 72 x 60.
Lent by the artist.

**Descending Arrow.** 1956.
Oil on canvas. 96 x 72.
Lent by the artist.

**The Frozen Sounds, Number I.** 1951.
Oil on canvas. 36 x 48.
Whitney Museum of American Art.
   Gift of Mr. and Mrs. Samuel M. Kootz.

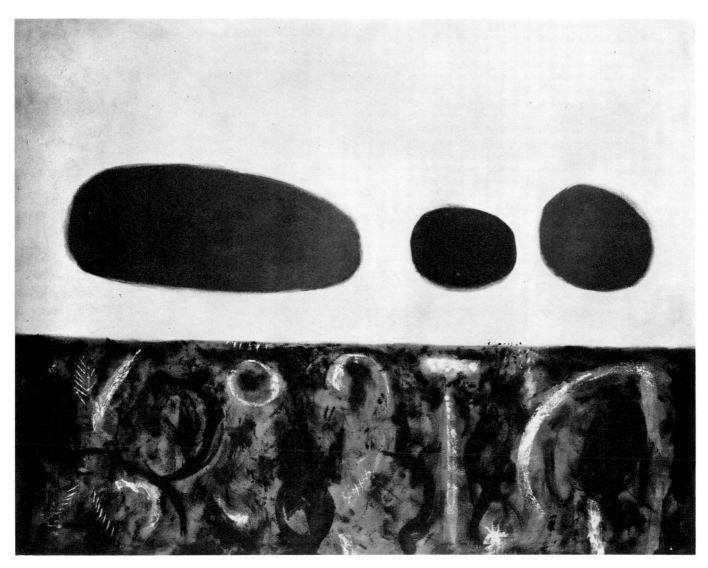

**Sea and Tide.** 1952.
Oil on canvas. 60 x 72.
Lent by the artist.

**Nadir.** 1952.
Oil on canvas. 42 x 72.
Lent by the artist.

**Side Pull.** 1956.
Oil on canvas. 50 x 60.
Lent by Mr. Clement Greenberg.

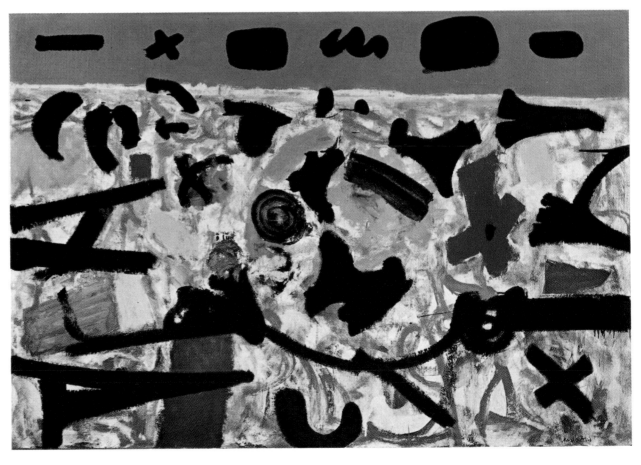

**Hot Horizon.** 1956.
Oil on canvas. 72 x 96.
Lent by Mr. Charles B. Benenson.

**Blue at Night.** 1957.
Oil on canvas. 42 x 60.
Lent by The Virginia Museum of Fine Arts.

**Exclamation.** 1958.
Oil on canvas. 90 x 72.
Lent by Mrs. Adolph Gottlieb.

**Tan over Black.** 1958.
Oil on canvas. 108 x 90.
Lent by the artist.

**Transfiguration Number 3.** 1958.
Oil on canvas. 90 x 60.
Lent by Mr. William S. Rubin.

**Jagged.** 1960.
Oil on canvas. 72 x 48.
Lent by Colonel Samuel A. Berger.

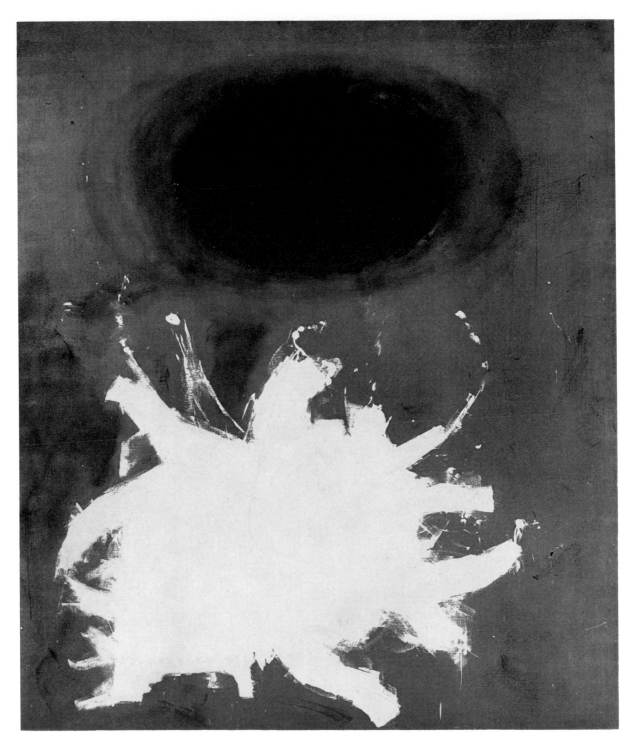

**The Crest.** 1959.
Oil on canvas. 108$\frac{1}{4}$ x 90$\frac{1}{4}$.
Whitney Museum of American Art. Gift of The
  Chase Manhattan Bank.

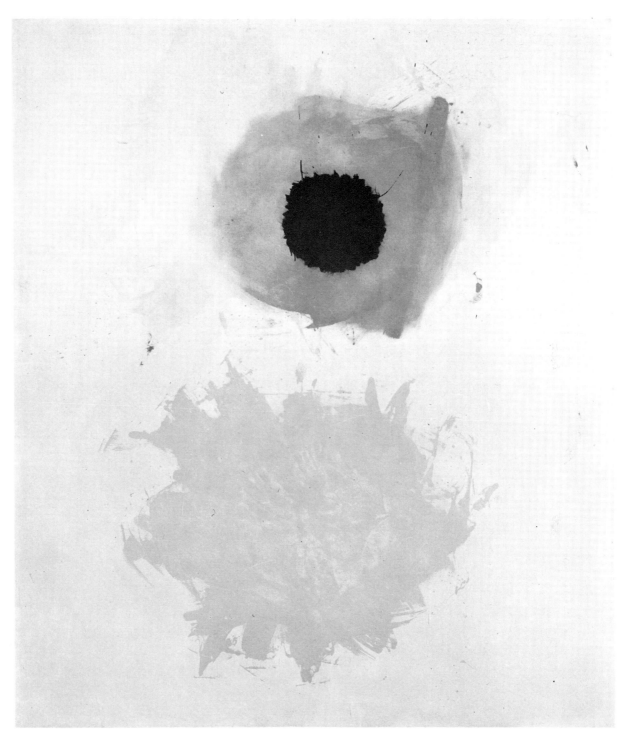

**Aureole. 1959.**
Oil on canvas. 108 x 90.
Lent by the artist.

**Black Black.** 1961.
Oil on canvas. 72 x 60.
Lent by The Community Synagogue of Sands Point.

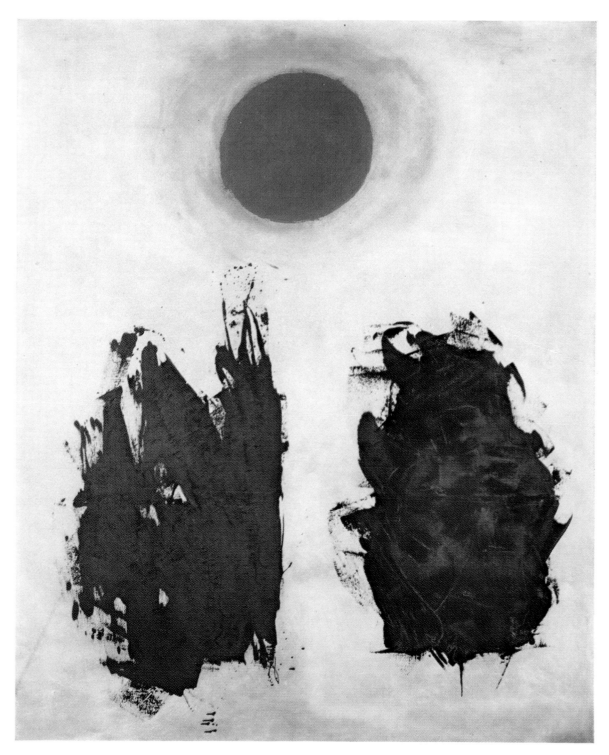

**Triad.** 1959.
Oil on canvas. 90 x 72.
Lent by Mr. and Mrs. Alexander Lerner.

**Rising.** 1961.
Oil on canvas. 72$^{1}/_{8}$ x 48.
Lent by Brandeis University Art Collection.
  Gevirtz-Mnuchin Purchase Fund.

**Mist.** 1961.
Oil on canvas. 72 x 48.
Lent by Mrs. Frederick W. Hilles.

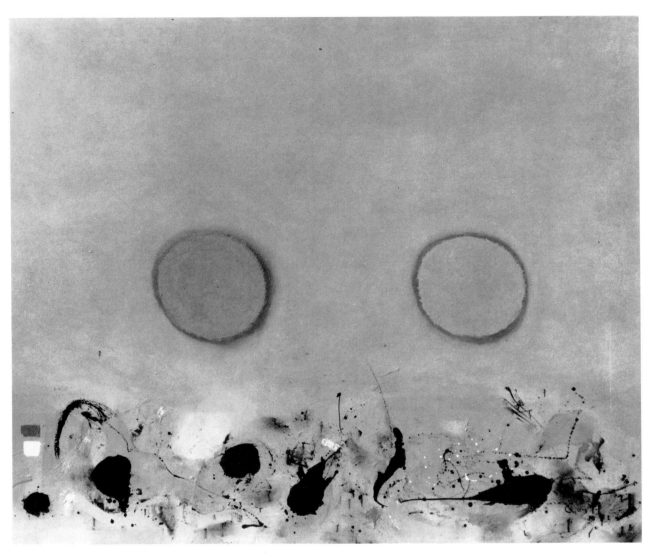

**Two Discs.** 1963.
Oil on canvas. 90 x 108.
Lent by the Joseph H. Hirshhorn Collection.

**Rolling.** 1961.
Oil on canvas. 90 x 72.
Lent by Mr. and Mrs. A. I. Sherr.

**Duet.** 1962.
Oil on canvas. 84 x 90.
Lent by The High Museum of Art. Gift of Governor
    Nelson A. Rockefeller, 1963.

**Expanding.** 1962.
Oil on canvas. 90 x 72.
Lent by The Art Institute of Chicago.

**Dialogue Number 1.** 1960.
Oil on canvas. 66 x 132.
Lent by the Albright-Knox Art Gallery.

**Return.** 1962.
Oil on canvas. 48 x 72.
Lent by The Larry Aldrich Museum.

**Winsor Green Field.** 1962.
Oil on canvas. 36 x 48.
Lent by Mr. J. Frederic Byers III.

**Sign.** 1962.
Oil on canvas. 90 x 60.
Lent by the artist, courtesy of Marlborough-
  Gerson Gallery, New York.

**Trinity.** 1962.
Oil on canvas. 80 x 185.
Lent by Mr. W. Hawkins Ferry.

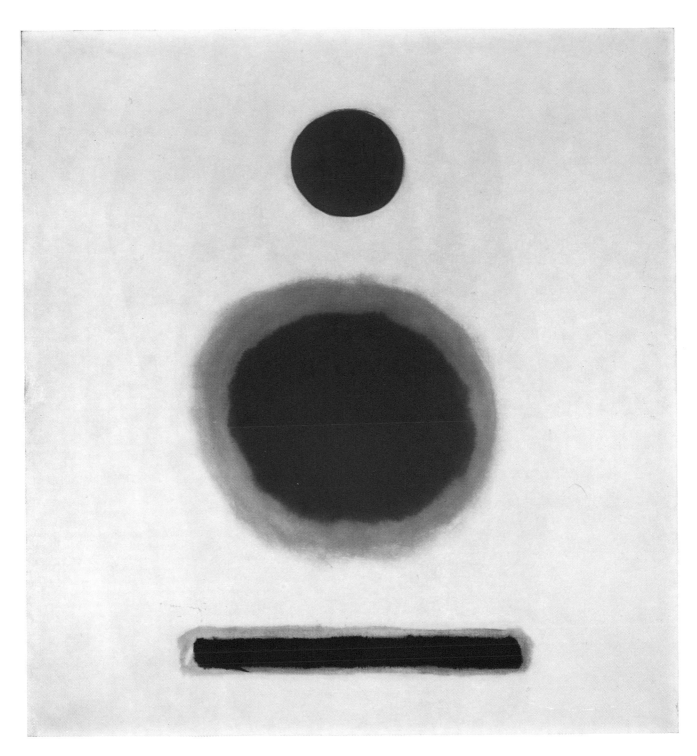

**Ping.** 1964.
Oil on canvas. 90 x 84.
Lent by the artist, courtesy of Marlborough-
  Gerson Gallery, New York.

**Orb.** 1964.
Oil on canvas. 90 x 60.
Lent by The Dallas Museum of Fine Arts.

**Above and Below I.** 1964-65.
Oil on canvas. 90 x 108.
Lent by the artist, courtesy of Marlborough-
    Gerson Gallery, New York.

**Excalibur.** 1963.
Oil on canvas. 84 x 90.
Whitney Museum of American Art. Gift of the
    Friends of the Whitney Museum of American Art
    (and purchase).

**Smolder.** 1964.
Oil on canvas. 73 x 42.
Lent by Mr. George T. Lee, Jr.

**Focal.** 1965.
Oil on canvas. 90 x 72.
Lent by The Joan and Lester Avnet Collection.

**Conflicts.** 1966.
Oil on canvas. 72 x 90.
Lent by the Flint Institute of Arts.

**Azimuth.** 1965.
Oil on canvas. 96 x 144.
Lent by the artist, courtesy of Marlborough-
  Gerson Gallery, New York.

**Units III.** 1965.
Oil & acrylic on canvas. 96 x 144.
Lent by the artist, courtesy of Marlborough-
  Gerson Gallery, New York.

**Units II.** 1965.
Oil & acrylic on canvas. 96 x 144.
Lent by the artist, courtesy of Marlborough-
    Gerson Gallery, New York.

**Glow.** 1966.
Oil on canvas. 90 x 72.
Lent by the artist, courtesy of Marlborough-
   Gerson Gallery, New York.

**Green Haze.** 1966.
Oil on canvas. 72 x 90.
Lent by the artist, courtesy of Marlborough-
  Gerson Gallery, New York.

**Red, Blue, Yellow.** 1966.
Oil on canvas. 84 x 90.
Lent by the artist, courtesy of Marlborough-
    Gerson Gallery, New York.

## catalogue of the exhibition

The arrangement is chronological. Measurements are in inches, height preceding width. Works marked with an asterisk are illustrated. Works marked with a dagger are shown in New York only. **Rolling,** lent by Mr. and Mrs. A. I. Sherr, is shown in New York and Washington, D.C. only. Numbers 1 through 59 are shown at The Solomon R. Guggenheim Museum. Numbers 60 through 127 are shown at the Whitney Museum of American Art.

1 **Eyes of Oedipus.** 1941.*
Oil on canvas. 32 x 25.
Lent by Mrs. Adolph Gottlieb.

2 **Pictograph Symbol.** 1942.
Oil on canvas. 54 x 40.
Lent by Mrs. Adolph Gottlieb.

3 **Pictograph.** 1942.*
Oil on canvas. 48 x 36.
Lent by the artist.

4 **The Red Bird.** 1944.*
Oil on canvas. 40 x 30.
The Solomon R. Guggenheim Museum.

5 **Compartments of Silence.** 1945.
Oil on canvas. 25 x 17.
The Solomon R. Guggenheim Museum.

6 **Expectation of Evil.** 1945.*
Oil on canvas. 43 x 27.
Lent by the artist.

7 **The Alkahest of Paracelsus.** 1945.*
Oil on canvas. 60 x 44.
Lent by the artist.

8 **Pendant Image.** 1946.*
Oil on canvas. 25 x 32.
The Solomon R. Guggenheim Museum.

9 **Recurrent Apparition.** 1946.*
Oil on canvas. 36 x 54.
Lent by the artist.

10 **Pictograph.** 1946.*
Oil on canvas. 36 x 48.
Lent by Mrs. Martha Jackson.

11 **Black Enigma.** 1946.*
Oil on canvas. 28 x 34.
Lent by Mr. and Mrs. Lawrence Richmond.

†12 **Evil Omen.** 1946.*
Oil on canvas. 38 x 30.
Lent by Mr. and Mrs. Roy R. Neuberger.

13 **Links of Memory.** 1946.
Oil on canvas. 40 x 36.
Lent by Mr. and Mrs. Harvey Probber.

14 **Pictogenic Fragments.** 1946.*
Oil on canvas. 36 x 30.
Lent by the Joseph H. Hirshhorn Collection.

15 **Totem.** 1947.
Oil on canvas. 48 x 36.
Lent by Dr. and Mrs. Norman Laskey.

16 **Oracle.** 1947.*
Oil on canvas. 60 x 44.
Lent by Mr. and Mrs. Albert A. List.

†17 **Sorceress.** 1947.*
Oil on canvas. 48 x 36.
Lent by Columbia University. Gift of Mr. and Mrs. Samuel M. Kootz.

18 **Water, Air, Fire.** 1947.*
Oil on pressed board. 30 x 24.
Lent by Brandeis University Art Collection. Gift of Mr. and Mrs. Samuel M. Kootz.

19 **Altar.** 1947.*
Oil on canvas. 48 x 36.
Lent by Mr. and Mrs. Samuel M. Kootz.

†20 **Pursuer and Pursued.** 1947.*
Oil on canvas. 38 x 36.
Lent by Yale University Art Gallery. Gift of Fred Olsen.

†21 **Geometry of Hallucination.** 1947.
Oil on canvas. 24 x 30.
Lent by Mr. and Mrs. Roy R. Neuberger.

22 **Sorcerer.** 1948.*
Oil on canvas. 38 x 30.
Lent by Mr. Harold Diamond.

23 **Vigil.** 1948.*
Oil on canvas. 36 x 48.
Lent by the Whitney Museum of American Art.

24 **Dream.** 1948.*
Oil on canvas. 20 x 24.
Lent by the Isaac Delgado Museum of Art. Gift of William March Campbell.

25 **Sounds at Night.** 1948.*
Oil on canvas. 48 x 60.
Lent by the artist.

26 **Bent Arrow.** 1949.*
Oil on canvas. 36 x 48.
Lent by Mr. and Mrs. Boris N. Greenberg.

27 **Romanesque Facade.** 1949.*
Oil on canvas. 48 x 36.
Lent by the Krannert Art Museum, University of Illinois.

†28 **Man Looking at Woman.** 1949.*
Oil on canvas. 42 x 54.
Lent by Mr. William S. Rubin.

29 **Man Looking at Woman II.** 1949.
Oil on canvas. 48 x 36.
Lent by Mr. and Mrs. Harvey Probber.

30 **Hidden Image.** 1950.*
Oil on canvas. 42 x 54.
Lent by the artist.

†31 **The Seer.** 1950.*
Oil on canvas. 60 x 72.
Lent by The Phillips Collection.

32 **Man and Arrow I.** 1950.
Oil and canvas. 42 x 54.
Lent by the artist.

33 **Man and Arrow II.** 1950.*
Oil on canvas. 38 x 30.
Lent by Mrs. Adolph Gottlieb.

34 **Male and Female.** 1950.*
Oil on burlap. 48 x 60.
Lent by the artist.

†35 **T.** 1950.*
Oil on canvas. 48 x 36.
Lent by The Metropolitan Museum of Art.
David M. and Hope G. Solinger Foundation,
Inc., Gift Fund, 1952.

36 **Archer.** 1951.*
Oil on canvas. 72 x 60.
Lent by the artist.

37 **Figuration of Clangor.** 1951.*
Oil on canvas. 48 x 60.
Lent by the artist.

38 **E.** 1951.
Oil on canvas. 48 x 36.
Lent by Mrs. Adolph Gottlieb.

39 **Untitled.** 1951.*
Oil on canvas. 48 x 60.
Lent by Mr. and Mrs. Harvey Probber.

†40 **Figure.** 1951.*
Oil on canvas. 24 x 20.
Lent by Mr. and Mrs. David M. Solinger.

41 **Sentinel.** 1951.*
Oil on canvas. 60 x 48.
Lent by the artist.

42 **Tournament.** 1951.*
Oil on canvas. 60 x 72.
Lent by Mrs. Adolph Gottlieb.

43 **Symbols and a Woman.** 1951.*
Oil on canvas. 60 x 72.
Lent by the artist.

†44 **Ebb Tide.** 1951.*
Oil on canvas. 24 x 30.
Private collection.

45 **Unstill Life.** 1952.*
Oil on canvas. 36 x 48.
Lent by the Whitney Museum of American Art.
Gift of Mr. and Mrs. Alfred Jaretzki, Jr.

46 **Trajectory.** 1954.*
Oil on canvas. 40 x 50.
Lent by Mr. and Mrs. Robert A. Rowan.

47 **Labyrinth III.** 1954.*
Oil on canvas. 84 x 192.
Lent by the artist.

48 **Armature.** 1954.
Oil on canvas. 50 x 40.
Lent by Dr. Morton M. Kligerman.

49 **The Couple.** 1955.
Oil on canvas. 72 x 60.
Lent by the artist.

50 **Blue at Noon.** 1955.*
Oil on canvas. 60 x 72.
Lent by the Walker Art Center.

51 **Composition.** 1955.*
Oil on canvas. 72 x 60.
Lent by the artist.

52 **Unstill Life III.** 1954-56.
Oil on canvas. 80 x 185.
Lent by The Museum of Modern Art.
Given anonymously.

53 **Descending Arrow.** 1956.*
Oil on canvas. 96 x 72.
Lent by the artist.

WORKS ON PAPER

54 **Disparate Images.** 1945.
Gouache on paper. 21 x 28.
Lent by Mrs. Adolph Gottlieb.

55 **The Centers of Lateral Resistance.** 1945.
Gouache on paper. 32 x 22.
The Solomon R. Guggenheim Museum.

56 **Sleep Mask.** 1945.
Tempera with pencil on paper. 26 x 20.
The Solomon R. Guggenheim Museum.

57 **Ancestral Figures.** 1946.
Gouache on paper. 26 x 20.
Lent by Mr. Benjamin Baldwin.

58 **Incubus.** 1947.
Gouache on paper. 23 x 17.
Lent by The North Carolina Museum of Art.
Bequest of W. R. Valentiner.

59 **Sacred Rites.** n.d.
Gouache on paper. 31 x 22.
Lent by Mr. Benjamin Baldwin.

60 **The Frozen Sounds, Number 1.** 1951.*
Oil on canvas. 36 x 48.
Whitney Museum of American Art. Gift of
    Mr. and Mrs. Samuel M. Kootz.

61 **Nadir.** 1952.*
Oil on canvas. 42 x 72.
Lent by the artist.

62 **Sea and Tide.** 1952.*
Oil on canvas. 60 x 72.
Lent by the artist.

63 **Water and Sound.** 1952.
Oil on canvas. 60 x 72.
Lent by the artist.

64 **From Midnight to Dawn.** 1956.
Oil on canvas. 72 x 96.
Lent by the artist.

†65 **Groundscape.** 1956.
Oil on canvas. 84 x 144.
Lent by Mrs. Adolph Gottlieb.

†66 **Hot Horizon.** 1956.*
Oil on canvas. 72 x 96.
Lent by Mr. Charles B. Benenson.

67 **Red at Night.** 1956.
Oil on canvas. 72 x 96.
Lent by the artist.

68 **Side Pull.** 1956.*
Oil on canvas. 50 x 60.
Lent by Mr. Clement Greenberg.

69 **Blast II.** 1957.
Oil on canvas. 90 x 45.
Lent by Joseph E. Seagram & Sons, Inc.

70 **Blue at Night.** 1957.*
Oil on canvas. 42 x 60.
Lent by The Virginia Museum of Fine Arts.

71 **Burst.** 1957.*
Oil on canvas. 96 x 40.
Lent by Mr. and Mrs. Ben Heller.

†72 **Exclamation.** 1958.*
Oil on canvas. 90 x 72.
Lent by Mrs. Adolph Gottlieb.

73 **Tan over Black.** 1958.*
Oil on canvas. 108 x 90.
Lent by the artist.

†74 **Transfiguration Number 1.** 1958.
Oil on canvas. 90 x 60.
Private collection.

†75 **Transfiguration Number 3.** 1958.*
Oil on canvas. 90 x 60.
Lent by Mr. William S. Rubin.

76 **Aureole.** 1959.*
Oil on canvas. 108 x 90.
Lent by the artist.

77 **The Crest.** 1959.*
Oil on canvas. 108$\frac{1}{4}$ x 90$\frac{1}{4}$.
Whitney Museum of American Art. Gift of
    The Chase Manhattan Bank.

†78 **Crimson Spinning.** 1959.
Oil on canvas. 90 x 72.
Private collection.

79 **Triad.** 1959.*
Oil on canvas. 90 x 72.
Lent by Mr. and Mrs. Alexander Lerner.

80 **Una.** 1959.
Oil on canvas. 108 x 90.
Lent by the artist.

†81 **Dialogue Number 1.** 1960.*
Oil on canvas. 66 x 132.
Lent by the Albright-Knox Art Gallery.

82 **Jagged.** 1960.*
Oil on canvas. 72 x 48.
Lent by Colonel Samuel A. Berger.

83 **Black Black.** 1961.*
Oil on canvas. 72 x 60.
Lent by The Community Synagogue of
    Sands Point.

†84 **Mist.** 1961.*
Oil on canvas. 72 x 48.
Lent by Mrs. Frederick W. Hilles.

85 **Rolling.** 1961.*
Oil on canvas. 90 x 72.
Lent by Mr. and Mrs. A. I. Sherr.

†86 **Duet.** 1962.*
Oil on canvas. 84 x 90.
Lent by The High Museum of Art. Gift of Gov-
    ernor Nelson A. Rockefeller, 1963.

†87 **Expanding.** 1962.*
Oil on canvas. 90 x 72.
Lent by The Art Institute of Chicago.

†88 **Return.** 1962.*
Oil on canvas. 48 x 72.
Lent by The Larry Aldrich Museum.

89 **Rising.** 1962.*
Oil on canvas. 72$\frac{1}{8}$ x 48.
Lent by Brandeis University Art Collection.
    Gevirtz-Mnuchin Purchase Fund.

90 **Sign.** 1962.*
Oil on canvas. 90 x 60.
Lent by the artist, courtesy of Marlborough-
    Gerson Gallery, New York.

†91 **Trinity.** 1962.*
Oil on canvas. 80 x 185.
Lent by Mr. W. Hawkins Ferry.

†92 **Winsor Green Field.** 1962.*
Oil on canvas. 36 x 48.
Lent by Mr. J. Frederic Byers III.

93 **Excalibur.** 1963.*
Oil on canvas. 84 x 90.
Whitney Museum of American Art. Gift of the Friends of the Whitney Museum of American Art (and purchase).

†94 **Two Discs.** 1963.*
Oil on canvas. 90 x 108.
Lent by the Joseph H. Hirshhorn Collection.

95 **Above and Below I.** 1964-65.*
Oil on canvas. 90 x 108.
Lent by the artist, courtesy of Marlborough-Gerson Gallery, New York.

96 **Azimuth.** 1965.*
Oil on canvas. 96 x 144.
Lent by the artist, courtesy of Marlborough-Gerson Gallery, New York.

97 **Equal.** 1964.*
Oil on canvas. 20 x 16.
Lent by Mr. Jack H. Klein.

98 **Icon.** 1964.
Oil & acrylic on canvas. 144 x 100.
Lent by the artist, courtesy of Marlborough-Gerson Gallery, New York.

†99 **Orb.** 1964.*
Oil on canvas. 90 x 60.
Lent by The Dallas Museum of Fine Arts.

100 **Ping.** 1964.*
Oil on canvas. 90 x 84.
Lent by the artist, courtesy of Marlborough-Gerson Gallery, New York.

†101 **Smolder.** 1964.*
Oil on canvas. 73 x 42.
Lent by Mr. George T. Lee, Jr.

102 **Focal.** 1965.*
Oil on canvas. 90 x 72.
Lent by The Joan and Lester Avnet Collection.

103 **Units II.** 1965.*
Oil & acrylic on canvas. 96 x 144.
Lent by the artist, courtesy of Marlborough-Gerson Gallery, New York.

104 **Units III.** 1965.*
Oil & acrylic on canvas. 96 x 144.
Lent by the artist, courtesy of Marlborough-Gerson Gallery, New York.

†105 **Conflicts.** 1966.*
Oil on canvas. 72 x 90.
Lent by the Flint Institute of Arts.

106 **Glow.** 1966.*
Oil on canvas. 90 x 72.
Lent by the artist, courtesy of Marlborough-Gerson Gallery, New York.

107 **Green Haze.** 1966.*
Oil on canvas. 72 x 90.
Lent by the artist, courtesy of Marlborough-Gerson Gallery, New York.

108 **Red, Blue, Yellow.** 1966.*
Oil on canvas. 84 x 90.
Lent by the artist, courtesy of Marlborough-Gerson Gallery, New York.

WORKS ON PAPER

109 **Burst Number 4.** 1965.
Acrylic on paper. 24 x 19.
Lent by the artist, courtesy of Marlborough-Gerson Gallery, New York.

110 **Untitled.** 1965.
Acrylic on paper. 20 x 26.
Lent by the artist, courtesy of Marlborough-Gerson Gallery, New York.

111 **Untitled.** 1966.
Acrylic on paper. 19 x 24.
Lent by the artist, courtesy of Marlborough-Gerson Gallery, New York.

112 **Untitled.** 1966.
Acrylic on paper. 24 x 19.
Lent by the artist, courtesy of Marlborough-Gerson Gallery, New York.

113 **Untitled.** 1966.
Acrylic on paper. 20 x 26.
Lent by the artist, courtesy of Marlborough-Gerson Gallery, New York.

114 **Untitled.** 1967.
Oil on paper. 19 x 24.
Lent by the artist, courtesy of Marlborough-Gerson Gallery, New York.

GRAPHICS

115 **Black Ground-Red Disc.** 1966.
Serigraph. $28^1/_2$ x 20.
Lent by Mr. and Mrs. Barney Weinger.

116 **Chrome Yellow-Green Disc.** 1966.
Lithograph. 30 x 22.
Lent by Mr. and Mrs. Barney Weinger.

117 **Green Ground-Black Form.** 1966.
Lithograph. 30 x 22.
Lent by Mr. and Mrs. Barney Weinger.

118 **Green Ground-Blue Disc.** 1966.
Serigraph. 24 x 18.
Lent by Mr. and Mrs. Barney Weinger.

119 **Green Halo,** 1966.
Serigraph. 24 x 18.
Lent by Mr. and Mrs. Barney Weinger.

120 **Lemon Yellow Ground.** 1966.
Serigraph. 20 x 28$^1$/$_2$.
Lent by Mr. and Mrs. Barney Weinger.

121 **Magenta Disc.** 1966.
Serigraph. 24 x 18.
Lent by Mr. and Mrs. Barney Weinger.

122 **Red Ground-Maroon Disc.** 1966.
Serigraph. 24 x 18.
Lent by Mr. and Mrs. Barney Weinger.

123 **Red Halo-White Ground.** 1966.
Serigraph. 24 x 18.
Lent by Mr. and Mrs. Barney Weinger.

124 **White Ground-Red Disc.** 1966.
Lithograph. 30 x 22.
Lent by Mr. and Mrs. Barney Weinger.

POSTCARDS

†125 **Musée Guimet, Devinette Féminine.** 1962.
Magna color on paper. 5$^1$/$_2$ x 3$^3$/$_4$.
Lent by Mrs. Samuel Weiner.

†126 **Watteau, assemblée dans un parc.** 1963.
Magna color on paper. 3$^1$/$_2$ x 5.
Lent by Mr. and Mrs. Bernard Rosenthal.

†127 **Musée Guimet, Cheval & Cavalier.** 1963.
Magna color on paper. 5$^1$/$_2$ x 3$^1$/$_2$.
Lent by the artist.

## public collections

Addison Gallery of American Art, Andover, Massachusetts
Albright-Knox Art Gallery, Buffalo, New York
The Art Institute of Chicago
Ball State Teachers College Art Gallery, Muncie, Indiana
Bezalel Museum, Jerusalem
Brandeis University Art Collection, Waltham, Massachusetts
The Brooklyn Museum, New York
Butler Institute of American Art, Youngstown, Ohio
Carnegie Institute, Museum of Art, Pittsburgh, Pennsylvania
Columbia University, New York
The Corcoran Gallery of Art, Washington, D.C.
The Dallas Museum of Fine Arts
Isaac Delgado Museum of Art, New Orleans, Louisiana
Des Moines Art Center
The Detroit Institute of Arts
Flint Institute of Arts, Flint, Michigan
The Solomon R. Guggenheim Museum, New York
The High Museum of Art, Atlanta, Georgia
The Jewish Museum, The Jewish Theological Seminary of America, New York
Krannert Art Museum, University of Illinois, Urbana, Illinois
Los Angeles County Museum of Art
Joe and Emily Lowe Art Gallery, University of Miami, Coral Gables, Florida
The Metropolitan Museum of Art, New York
The Museum of Modern Art, New York
Munson-Williams-Proctor Institute, Utica, New York
The University of Nebraska Art Galleries, Lincoln, Nebraska
University of Nevada, Reno, Nevada
The Newark Museum
New York University
The North Carolina Museum of Art, Raleigh, North Carolina
The Phillips Collection, Washington, D.C.
Smith College Museum of Art, Northampton, Massachusetts
Society of the Four Arts, Palm Beach, Florida
Tel Aviv Museum, Israel
Victoria & Albert Museum, London
Virginia Museum of Fine Arts, Richmond
Wadsworth Atheneum, Hartford, Connecticut
Walker Art Center, Minneapolis, Minnesota
Andrew Dickson White Museum of Art, Cornell University, Ithaca, New York
Whitney Museum of American Art, New York
Yale University Art Gallery, New Haven, Connecticut

## chronology

1903   Born March 14, New York City.

1920   Left high school and enrolled at the Art Students League. Studied under John Sloan and Robert Henri.

1921   Worked his passage to Europe. Attended sketch classes at the Académie de la Grande Chaumière, Paris, and other studio schools, visited the museums extensively and travelled to Berlin and Munich.

1923   Returned to New York City. Finished high school and studied at Parsons School of Design, The Art Students League, Cooper Union, and the Educational Alliance Art School. His efforts devoted only to painting, he supported himself by part-time jobs.

1929   Awarded a joint-prize in the Dudensing National Competition.

1930   Shared an exhibition at the Dudensing Galleries, New York with Konrad Cramer.

1932   Married Esther Dick.

1935   Spent two months in Europe. Became a founding member of "The Ten," a group united by their devotion to expressionist and abstract painting. It included Ilya Bolotowsky, Lee Gatch and Mark Rothko. They exhibited annually until 1940. Began to collect primitive sculpture.

1936   Employed as an easel painter on WPA Federal Art Project.

1937   Moved to the desert near Tucson, Arizona.

1939   Returned to New York. Began to spend summers in Gloucester, Massachusetts, with Milton Avery. Became an avid sailor. Won U.S. Treasury sponsored nationwide mural competition. Commissioned to paint a mural in the Yerrington, Nevada, Post Office.

1941   Began to develop the *Pictographs.*

1944   Awarded First Prize, Brooklyn Society of Artists, Annual Exhibition.

1944-45   President of the Federation of Modern Painters and Sculptors.

1946   Participated in a forum, "Problems of Art and Artists Today and Tomorrow," sponsored by The Art Students League and The Federation of Modern Painters and Sculptors, Inc. Began to spend summers in Provincetown, Massachusetts.

1948   Participated in a forum, "The Modern Artist Speaks," at The Museum of Modern Art.

1949   Participated in a forum, "The Schism Between Artist and Public," sponsored by The Art Students League and The Federation of Modern Painters and Sculptors, Inc.

1951   Designed the ark curtain for Congregation B'nai Israel, Millburn, New Jersey. Received a purchase prize, University of Illinois, Contemporary American Painting.

1952   Designed and supervised fabrication of a 1,300 square-foot stained glass facade for The Milton Steinberg Memorial Center, New York City. *The Frozen Sounds, Number I* shown at Kootz Gallery, New York. First of the Imaginary Landscapes.

1953   Designed the ark curtain for Congregation Beth El, Springfield, Massachusetts.

1954   Participated in a conference, "Art Education and the Creative Process," sponsored by The Museum of Modern Art.

1957   *Burst* shown at The Jewish Museum, New York. First in a series of the same title.

1958   Taught at Pratt Institute, Brooklyn, New York, and at the University of California at Los Angeles, Los Angeles, California.

1960   Moved to East Hampton, Long Island, New York.

1961   Awarded Third Prize, Pittsburgh International Exhibition, Carnegie Institute.

1963   Awarded Grand Premio, VII Bienal de São Paulo, Brazil.

1965   Received award, American Academy of Achievement, Dallas, Texas.

1966   Studio and contents destroyed by fire.

1967   Appointed to The Art Commission, City of New York. Lives in New York City and East Hampton, Long Island, New York.

# exhibitions

1930 Dudensing Galleries, New York, May

1934 Uptown Gallery, New York, February
   Theodore A. Kohn & Son, New York, May

1940 Artists Gallery, New York, April 16-30

1942 Artists Gallery, New York, December 28-January 11, 1943*

1944 Wakefield Gallery, New York, February 7-19*

1945 Gallery 67, New York, March 12-31*
   Nierendorf Galleries, New York, December

1947 Kootz Gallery, New York, January 6-25*
   Kootz Gallery, New York, November 3-24

1949 Jacques Seligmann Galleries, New York, January 24-February 12*

1950 Kootz Gallery, New York, January 10-31*

1951 Kootz Gallery, New York, January 2-22

1952 Kootz Gallery, New York, January 8-26*

1953 Kootz Gallery, New York, January 5-24*
   Area Arts, San Francisco, March 3-31

1954 Kootz Gallery, New York, April 5-24*
   Bennington College, Bennington, Vermont, April 23-May 5; Williams
    College, Williamstown, Massachusetts, May 7-23*
   Kootz Gallery, Provincetown, Massachusetts, August 7-20

1957 Martha Jackson Gallery, New York, January 29-February 23
   HCE Gallery, Provincetown, Massachusetts, August
   The Jewish Museum, New York, November 17-December 31*

1958 André Emmerich Gallery, New York, January 3-31*

1959 André Emmerich Gallery, New York, January 5-31
   Galerie Rive Droite, Paris, April 3-30; Institute of Contemporary Arts, London, June*
   Paul Kantor Gallery, Beverly Hills, April 27-May 23*

1960 French and Company, Inc., New York, January*
   Sidney Janis Gallery, New York, November 7-December 3

1961 Galleria dell' Ariete, Milan, May*
   Galerie Handschin, Basel, September-October 10*

1962 Sidney Janis Gallery, New York, October 1-27

1963 Walker Art Center, Minneapolis, April 28-June 9; American Section of
    VII Bienal de São Paulo, September-December*

1964 Marlborough-Gerson Gallery, New York, February 13-March 3*

1966 Marlborough-Gerson Gallery, New York, February 16-March 15*
   Hayden Gallery, Massachusetts Institute of Technology, Cambridge,
    Massachusetts, May 7-June 12*

1967 The Arts Club of Chicago, May 22-June 23*
   The Solomon R. Guggenheim Museum, New York, February 14-April 7*
   Whitney Museum of American Art, New York, February 14-March 31*

IMPORTANT GROUP EXHIBITIONS

1935 The Ten, Montross Gallery, New York, December

1936 The Ten, Montross Gallery, New York, December

1937 The Ten, Georgette Passedoit Gallery, New York, May

1938 The Ten, Georgette Passedoit Gallery, New York, May
        Mercury Galleries, New York, November

1939 The Ten, Bonestell Gallery, New York, October

1940 Loan Exhibition of Mural Designs for Federal Buildings from The Section of Fine Art,
    Washington, D. C.; Whitney Museum of American Art, New York, February 27-
    March 17

1943 Riverside Museum, American Modern Artists' Annual, February

1944 Abstract and Surrealist Art in America, Mortimer Brandt Gallery, New York,
    November 29-December 30

1945 A Painting Prophecy — 1950, The David Porter Gallery, Washington, D. C., February
    A Problem for Critics, 67 Gallery, New York, May 14-July 7

1946 American Painting from the Eighteenth Century to the Present Day, The Tate Gallery,
    London. Assembled by The National Gallery of Art, Washington, D. C.
    Advancing American Art, The Metropolitan Museum of Art, New York, October 4-18

1947 Introduction à la Peinture Moderne Américaine, Galerie Maeght, Paris, March-April
    Abstract and Surrealist American Art, The Art Institute of Chicago,
    November 6-January 11

1948 Third Anniversary Exhibition, Kootz Gallery, New York, March 29-April 17

1949 American Painting in Our Century, Institute of Contemporary Art, Boston,
    January 20-March 1
    The Intrasubjectives, Kootz Gallery, New York, September 14-October 3
    Juliana Force and American Art, Whitney Museum of American Art, New York,
    September 24-October 30
    Contemporary Art in Great Britain — United States — France, The Art Gallery of
    Toronto, November-December

1950 American Painting Today, Florida Gulf Coast Art Center, 1950, April
    American Painting 1950, Virginia Museum of Fine Arts, Richmond, April 22-June 4
    American Painting, Walker Art Center, Minneapolis, October 15-December 10

1951 Seventeen Modern American Painters, Frank Perls Gallery, Beverly Hills, California,
    January 11-February 7
    40 American Painters, 1940-50, University Gallery, University of Minnesota,
    Minneapolis, June 4-August 30
    American Vanguard Art for Paris, Sidney Janis Gallery, New York, December 26,
    1951-January 5, 1952; Regards sur la Peinture Américaine, Galerie de France,
    Paris, February 26-March 15, 1952

1952 Painters of Expressionist Abstractions, Phillips Gallery, Washington, D. C.,
    March 16-April 15
    Contemporary American Painting and Sculpture, Collection of Mr. and Mrs. Roy R.
    Neuberger, Walker Art Center, Minneapolis, May 24-August 10

1953 Origins and Trends of Contemporary Art, Denver Art Museum, January 11-February 15
    Exhibition: Adolph Gottlieb, Robert Motherwell, William Baziotes, Hans Hofmann,
    The Arts Club of Chicago, January 14-February 4; Walker Art Center, Minneapolis,
    February 15-March 15
    Provincetown-New York Artists, New School for Social Research, New York,
    March 3-17
    Art for a Synagogue, Kootz Gallery, New York, May 22-June 6

1954 Contemporary American Painting in honor of the American Jewish Tercentenary
1654-1955, Riverside Museum, New York, October 5-November 1954; William
Rockhill Nelson Gallery of Art, Kansas City, April 17-May 8
Younger American Painters, The Solomon R. Guggenheim Museum, New York,
May 12-July 25
Roy and Marie Neuberger Collection — Modern American Painting and Sculpture,
Whitney Museum of American Art, New York, November 17-December 19. Travelled
throughout United States.

1955 The New Decade — 35 American Painters and Sculptors, Whitney Museum of
American Art, New York, May 11-August 7. Travelled throughout United States
1955-1956

1956 Large Scale Paintings II, Contemporary Arts Association, Houston,
October 30-November 5

1957 Paintings from The Solomon R. Guggenheim Museum, New York, London, The Hague,
Helsinki, Rome, Cologne, Paris
American Paintings, 1945-1947, The Minneapolis Institute of Arts, June 18-September 1

1958 The New American Painting, Museum of Modern Art, International Council, New York
— Shown in eight European countries 1958-1959, with catalogue in the language of
the country: German, Dutch, Spanish, Italian, French
Nature in Abstraction, Whitney Museum of American Art, New York,
January 14-March 16; Travelled throughout United States 1958-1959
Action Painting . . . 1958, Dallas Museum for Contemporary Arts, Dallas,
March 5-April 13
The Museum and Its Friends, Whitney Museum of American Art, New York,
April 30-June 15

1959 Documenta II, Kassel, West Germany, July 11-October 11

1960 Contemporary American Painting, Columbus Gallery of Fine Arts, Columbus, Ohio,
January 14-February 18
Business Buys American Art, Whitney Museum of American Art, New York,
March 17-April 24
An American Group, Galerie Neufville, Paris, April
60 American Painters, 1960, Walker Art Center, Minneapolis, April 3-May 8
American Art 1910-1960, Selections from the Collection of Mr. and Mrs. Roy R.
Neuberger, M. Knoedler and Company, New York, June 8-September 9
Art Across America, Munson-Williams-Proctor Institute, Utica, New York,
October 15-December 31
The Mysterious Sign, Institute of Contemporary Arts, London, October 26-December 3

1961 Modern American Painting 1930-1958, USIS Gallery, American Embassy, London,
May 26-June 10
American Abstract Expressionists and Imagists, The Solomon R. Guggenheim
Museum, New York, October 13-December 31

1962 Selections 1934-1961, American Artists from the Collection of Martha Jackson,
Martha Jackson Gallery, New York, February 6-March 3
Art Since 1950, Fine Arts Pavillion, World's Fair, Seattle, April 21- October 21;
Institute of Contemporary Art, Boston, and Rose Art Museum, Brandeis University,
November 21-December 23
10 American Painters, Sidney Janis Gallery, New York, May 9-June 3

1963 Twenty-Six American Artists from The Collection of the Whitney Museum and Its
Friends, Whitney Museum of American Art, New York, July 16-September 8
Eleven Abstract Expressionist Painters, Sidney Janis Gallery, New York,
October 7-November 2

1964 Art Since 1945, Philadelphia Museum of Art
Guggenheim International Award 1964, The Solomon R. Guggenheim Museum,
New York, January, February, March

American Painting 1910 to 1960, Indiana University, Fine Arts Gallery, Bloomington,
  April 19-May 10
Painting and Sculpture of a Decade; 54-61, Tate Gallery, London, April 22-June 28
The Friends Collect, Whitney Museum of American Art, New York, May 8-June 16
Between the Fairs— 25 Years of American Art, Whitney Museum of American
  Art, New York, June 24-September 23
American Drawings, The Solomon R. Guggenheim Museum, New York, September-
  October
A Selection of 20th Century Art of 3 Generations, Sidney Janis Gallery, New York,
  November 24-December 26

1965  New York School The First Generation Paintings of the 1940's and 1950's,
        Los Angeles County Museum of Art, July 16-August 1

1966  Two Decades of American Painting, The Museum of Modern Art, International Council.
        Travelled to Japan, India, Australia, New South Wales 1966-1967
      Past and Present, Corcoran Gallery of Art, Washington D.C., April 15-September 15
      Seven Decades 1895-1965; Crosscurrents in Modern Art, Public Education
        Association, New York, April 26-May 21
      Art of The United States 1670-1966, Whitney Museum of American Art, New York,
        September 28-November 27
      The Media of Art: Now, University of Kentucky Art Gallery, Lexington,
        October 16-November 13
      Flint Invitational, Flint Institute of Arts, Flint, Michigan, November 4-December 31
      Abstract Expressionism — A Continuing Tradition, J. L. Hudson Gallery, Detroit,
        November 9-November 30

1967  White House Exhibition, Smithsonian Institution, Washington, D. C., January 1-
        December 15
      Contemporary Americans, Winnipeg Art Gallery, Canada, February
      The New York Painter: A Century of Teaching: Morse to Hofmann, Marlborough-
        Gerson Gallery, New York, September 27-October 14
      American Masters: Art Students League, American Federation of Arts,
        New York, October


PERIODIC EXHIBITIONS

The Art Institute of Chicago Annual: 1943, 1950, 1951, 1954, 1961, 1963, 1966

Brooklyn Museum Annual: 1944; Biennial: 1956

Corcoran Gallery of Art, Washington, D. C., Biennial: 1953, 1967

Denver Museum: 1957

University of Illinois, Urbana, Contemporary American Painting: 1948, 1950, 1951, 1952,
  1953, 1955, 1963

New Delhi, International Contemporary Art Exhibition: 1957

The Pennsylvania Academy of Fine Arts Annual: 1946, 1949, 1953, 1954

Pittsburgh International Exhibition, Carnegie Institute: 1952, 1955, 1958, 1961, 1964, 1967

Tokyo: International Art Exhibition: 1952, 1955

The Toledo Museum of Art: 1950

Whitney Museum of American Art, Annual Exhibition: 1940, 1941, 1944, 1945, 1946, 1947,
  1950, 1951, 1952, 1953, 1954, 1955, 1956, 1957, 1958, 1959, 1961, 1963, 1965, 1967

Wildenstein Galleries, Annual Exhibition of the Federation of Modern Painters and
  Sculptors: 1943, 1944, 1945, 1946

# bibliography

Compiled by Patricia FitzGerald Mandel

References are arranged alphabetically unless otherwise specified. Exhibition catalogues are listed under the name of the city in which the museum or gallery is located when not listed by author or exhibition title. The place of publication of books and exhibition catalogues is New York unless otherwise stated. Materials considered of secondary value, but accessible through standard reference works are not included.

ABBREVIATIONS

Ag August, Ap April, D December, F February, il illustration(s), Ja January, Je June, Jl July, Mr March, My May, N November, O October, p page(s), por portrait, S September.

GENERAL WORKS:

Armstrong, Richard: Abstract Expressionism Was an American Revolution. *Canadian Art* 21:262-265 S/O 1964.

Arnason, H. H.: *American Abstract Expressionists and Imagists,* The Solomon R. Guggenheim Museum, 1961.

*The Artist in America,* W. W. Norton & Company, 1967, p 200, 202, 1 il. Compiled by the Editors of *Art in America;* Introduction by Lloyd Goodrich.

Ashton, Dore: Perspective de la Peinture Américaine. *Cahiers d'Art* 33-35:203-220 1960. 1 il. Text in French.

———— La Signature américaine: *XX^e Siècle* no: 10:62-64 Mr 1958. Text in French.

———— *The Unknown Shore: A View of Contemporary Art,* Boston, Little, Brown and Company, 1962, p 25-26, 57-59. 1 il.

Baur, John I. H.: *Revolution and Tradition in Modern American Art,* Cambridge, Harvard University Press, 1954, p 72, 120, 143.

Blesh, Rudi: *Modern Art USA, Men, Rebellion, and Conquest, 1900-1956,* Alfred A. Knopf, 1956, p 266-267.

*Current Biography Yearbook,* ed., Charles Moritz, H. W. Wilson Co., 1959, p 155-156. por.

Davis, Stuart: Abstract Art in The American Scene. (In "Contemporary Painting") *Parnassus* 13:100-103 Mr 1941.

Donnell, Radka Zagaroff: Space in Abstract Expressionism. *Journal of Aesthetics* 23:239-249 Winter 1964.

Eliot, Alexander: *Three Hundred Years of American Painting,* Time Inc., 1957, p. 278, 1 il.

Feldman, Edmund Burke: *Art as Image and Idea,* Englewood Cliffs, N. J., Prentice-Hall, Inc., 1967, p 48, 179, 238, 254, 265. 1 il.

Ferentino, Effie: The American contribution to contemporary art. *New Forms* 1:70-72 Ja-F 1962.

Friedman, B. H.: The New Baroque. *Arts Digest* 28:12-13 S 15 1954.

Geldzahler, Henry: *American Painting in the Twentieth Century,* The Metropolitan Museum of Art, 1965, p 189-191, 215. 2 il.

Gollin, James M.: Gottlieb, *Art U.S.A. Now,* ed., lee Nordness, Lucerne, C. J. Bucher Ltd., 1962, v 1. 5 il., por.

Goodrich, Lloyd and Baur, John I. H.: *American Art of Our Century,* Frederick A. Praeger, 1961, p 211, 220. 1 il.

Goodrich, Lloyd: *Three Centuries of American Art,* Frederick A. Praeger, 1966, p 132. 1 il.

Greenberg, Clement: *Art and Culture, Critical Essays,* Boston, Beacon Press, 1961, p 216-217.

Haftmann, Werner: *Painting in The Twentieth Century,* Frederick A. Praeger, 1960, p 368. 1 il.

Hess, Thomas B.: *Abstract Painting,* Viking Press, 1951, p 122, 125, 145. 2 il.

Hunter, Sam: Abstract Expressionism Then — And Now. *Canadian Art* 21:266-269 S/O 1964.

_____ *Modern American Painting and Sculpture,* Dell, 1959, p 160. 1 il.

Janis, Sidney: *Abstract and Surrealist Art in America,* Reynal and Hitchcock, 1944, p 88. 1 il.

Kootz, Samuel M.: *New Frontiers in American Painting,* Hastings House, 1943, p 56. 1 il.

*The New York Painter,* New York University Art Collection, 1967, p 62, 86-87. 1 il.

*New York School The First Generation Paintings of the 1940's and 1950's,* ed., Maurice Tuchman, Los Angeles County Museum of Art, 1965, p 33-41, 89-98, 216-217. 8 il.

Pellegrini, Aldo: *New Tendencies in Art,* Crown, 1966, p 137-138, 214. 1 il.

Rose, Barbara: *American Art Since 1900: A Critical History,* Frederick A. Praeger, 1967, p 134, 163-164, 167, 197, 200-201, 207. 4 il.

Sawyer, Kenneth B.: The Century Plant: A Dialogue on Current Painting. *Hudson Review* 9:431-437 Autumn 1956.

Seeley, Carol: On The Nature of Abstract Painting in America. *(Magazine of Art* Essay Award) *Magazine of Art* 43:163-168 My 1950.

Wight, Frederick S.: *Milestones of American Painting in Our Century,* Chanticleer Press, 1949, p 106. 1 il.

STATEMENTS AND TEXTS BY GOTTLIEB (CHRONOLOGICALLY):

Gottlieb, Adolph and Rothko, Mark: In "The Realm of Art: A New Platform. 'Globalism' Pops into View," by Edward Alden Jewell, *New York Times* Je 13 1943, p 9. 1 il.

_____ The Portrait and The Modern Artist, O 13 1943, p 1-4. Mimeographed script of WNYC Broadcast: "Art in New York."

Gottlieb, Adolph: In A Painting Prophecy — 1950, Washington, D. C., The David Porter Gallery, 1945.

_____ In "Adolph Gottlieb," *Limited Edition* no. 5:4, 6 D 1945.

_____ Letter to Art Editor. *New York Times* Jl 22 1945.

_____ (In "The Ides of Art/The Attitudes of 10 Artists on their Art and Contemporaneousness") *The Tiger's Eye* 1:2:43 D 1947. 1 il (p 82).

_____ *Unintelligibility.* Mimeographed script from The Museum of Modern Art's Forum: The Artist Speaks, My 5 1948, p 1-4.

_____ (In "The Ides of Art/11 Graphic Artists Write") *The Tiger's Eye* 1:8:52 Je 1949. 1 il (p 28).

_____ *Selected Paintings by the late Arshile Gorky,* Kootz Gallery, 1950, p 2.

_____ In *American Vanguard Art for Paris,* Sidney Janis Gallery, 1951.

_____ In *40 American Painters, 1940 — 1950,* Minneapolis, University of Minnesota, 1951.

_____ In *Modern Artists in America,* ed., Robert Motherwell, Ad Reinhardt, Wittenborn-Schultz, 1951, Series I, p 9-10, 17-22. 1 il. Portions of statements used in *New York School The First Generation; Paintings of the 1940's and 1950's,* ed., Maurice Tuchman, Los Angeles County Museum of Art, 1965, p 33-41.

_____ My Painting. *Arts and Architecture* 68:21 S 1951. 2 il.

_____ In *Contemporary American Painting,* Urbana, University of Illinois, 1952, p 194. 1 il. Same statement as "40 American Painters," University of Minnesota, 1951.

_____ The Artist and the Public. *Art in America* 42:266-271 D 1954. 4 il. Talk presented to College Art Association Conference 1954.

_____ In *Contemporary American Painting and Sculpture,* Urbana, University of Illinois, 1955, p 202. 1 il.

_____ In *The New Decade: 35 American Painters and Sculptors,* ed., John I. H. Baur, Whitney Museum of American Art, 1955, p 34-36. 2 il.

_____ In "Integrating the Arts" *Interiors* 114:20, 171 Je 1955. por.

_____ Cover Design. (In "Letters to The Editor") *College Art Journal* 14:373 Summer 1955. 1 il.

_____ Artist and Society A Brief Case History. *College Art Journal* 14:96-101 Winter 1955, cover. Revised version of "The Artist and The Public," *Art in America* D 1954.

_____ In *Bradley Walker Tomlin* by John I. H. Baur, The Macmillan Company, 1957, p 26-28

_____ In *Conversations with Artists* by Selden Rodman, Devin-Adair, 1957, p 87-92.

_____ In *Nature in Abstraction* by John I. H. Baur, The Macmillan Company, 1958, p 58. 1 il (p 33).

_____ In *The New American Painting,* International Council at the Museum of Modern Art, 1959, p 36. 2 il, por.

_____ In "Stevenson Studying Abstract Art" by Gay Talese, *The New York Times* D 23 1959.

_____ Representational or Abstract? *Junior League Magazine* 50:6:2 N-D 1962.

_____ In "Adolph Gottlieb" *Estados Unidos da America,* São Paulo, VII Bienal do Museu de Arte Moderna, 1963, p 6-29, 22 il. Text in Portuguese and English.

_____ "Adolph Gottlieb: An Interview with David Sylvester" by David Sylvester, *Living Arts* 1:2-10 Je 1963. il.

_____ In "A New York Interview with Adolph Gottlieb" by Gordon Brown. *Art Voices* 3:12-13 F 1964. 5 il, por.

_____ Postcards from Adolph Gottlieb. *Location* 1:19-26 Summer 1964. il.

Gottlieb, Adolph and Sister Corita, I.H.M.: Art 1964. *Jubilee* 12:17-21 D 1964.

Gottlieb, Adolph: In "Jackson Pollock: An Artists' Symposium" *Art News* 66:31 Ap 1967.


EXHIBITION CATALOGUES DEVOTED TO GOTTLIEB:

Bennington, Vermont, Bennington College. *Adolph Gottlieb,* 1963. Introduction by Clement Greenberg.

Friedman, Martin: *Adolph Gottlieb,* Minneapolis, Walker Art Center, 1963, 48 pp. 29 il., por. Text used in: *Estados Unidos da America,* São Paulo, VII Bienal do Museu de Arte Moderna, 1963, p 5-30. 22 il., por.; *Adolph Gottlieb,* Marlborough-Gerson Gallery, 1964.

Greenberg, Clement: Adolph Gottlieb. *An Exhibition of Oil Paintings by Adolph Gottlieb,* The Jewish Museum, 1957, p 5-8. 9 il. Portions of text used: *Adolph Gottlieb, New Work,* André Emmerich Gallery, 1958, p 2. Complete text used for *Ecole de New York,* Paris, Galerie Rive Droite, 1959; *Adolph Gottlieb,* London, Institute of Contemporary Arts Gallery, 1959.

Kootz, Samuel M.: *Adolph Gottlieb,* Kootz Gallery, 1952, p 4. 3 il.

MacLeish, Archibald: *Imaginary Landscapes and Seascapes,* Kootz Gallery, 1953, p 3. 2 il., por.

Newman, Barnett: *Adolph Gottlieb,* Wakefield Gallery, 1944, p 2-3.

Stroup, Jon: *Adolph Gottlieb,* Gallery 67, 1945, p. 2.

Wolfson, Victor: *Adolph Gottlieb,* Kootz Gallery, 1947, p 2.


ARTICLES RELATED TO GOTTLIEB AND HIS EXHIBITIONS:

Alloway, Lawrence: The New American Painting. *Art International* 3:3-4:21-29 1959. 1 il.

_____ Paintings from the Big Country, *Art News and Review — U.S.A.* Special 11:4 Mr 14 1959, p 3. 1 il, cover.

_____ Sign and Surface: Notes on Black and White Painting in New York, *Quadrum,* no. 9:49-62 1960. 1 il.

Anon. Review: A Way to Kill Space. *Newsweek* 28:100, 106, 108 Ag 12 1946. 1 il.

_____ Adolph Gottlieb. (In "The Passing Shows") *Art News* 41:30 Ja 1-14 1943.

_____ Adolph Gottlieb. (In "The Passing Shows") *Art News* 43:23 F 15-29 1944.

_____ Adolph Gottlieb. (In "The Passing Shows") *Art News* 44:6 Ap 1-14 1945. 1 il.

_____ Adolph Gottlieb. (In "The Passing Shows") *Art News* 44:21 Ja 15-31 1946.

_____ Adolph Gottlieb. *Arts and Architecture* 63:26-28 Mr 1946. 4 il.

_____ Adolph Gottlieb's. (In "Reviews and Previews") *Art News* 45:45, 52 Ja 1947.

_____ Adolph Gottlieb. (In "Reviews and Previews") *Art News* 46:41-42 N 1947.

_____ American Abstraction Abroad. *Time* Ag 4 1958, p 40-45.

_____ Artist With Teeth. *Newsweek* D 31 1945, p 84, 86. 1 il.

_____ Austellungen, The Solomon R. Guggenheim Museum, New York: American Abstract Expressionists and Imagists, 1961. *Kunstwerk* 15:59 N-D 1961. 1 il.

_____ The Bienal's Best. *Time* 82:90 0 4 1963. por.

_____ Gottlieb & Oedipus Rex. *Art Digest* 17:10 Ja 1 1943.

_____ Gottlieb Wins Praise. *Arts Digest* 14:24 My 1 1940.

_____ Grande Premio Internacional de VII Bienal de São Paulo. *Habitat* no 74:65 D 1963. 1 il.

_____ Ivy on The Doric Column. *The Tiger's Eye* 1:3:100 Mr 15 1948. 1 il.

_____ Konrad Cramer, Adolph Gottlieb, Dudensing Galleries. *Art News* 28:15 My 17 1930.

_____ Modern Art for The Millburn Synagogue. *Magazine of Art* 44:216-217 O 1951. 1 il.

_____ The Muralist and The Modern Architect. *Arts and Architecture* 68:17-18 Ap 1951. 1 il.

_____ Oil Paintings by Adolph Gottlieb. *Irregular* p 40-41. il.

_____ Older. *Newsweek* 63:82 F 24 1964. il, por.

_____ Il Premio Carnegie 1961 vinto da Tobey e Giacometti. *Domus* no. 386:25 Ja 1962, 1 il.

_____ Sculpture and Tapestry Used Architecturally. *Architectural Forum* 100:141-145 Ap 1954. 13 il.

_____ Signs and Symbols: Decoration of the Millburn Synagogue. *Time* 58:87 N 19 1951. 1 il.

_____ Urbana Americana (In "Art news of America") *Art News* 50:8 Mr 1951, cover.

_____ Whitney & Force. *Time* O 3 1949 p 38. 1 il.

_____ Wild Ones. *Time* 67:70 F 20 1956.

_____ Young American Extremists, A Life Round Table on Modern Art. *Life* 25:62-63 O 11 1948. 1 il.

Ashton, Dore: (In "Art") *Arts and Architecture* 76:28-29 Mr 1959. 1 il (p 8).

_____ (In "High Tide For Assemblage: New York Commentary"). *Studio* 165: 26 Ja 1963. 1 il.

_____ (In "New York Letter") *Kunstwerk* 16:32 Ja 1963.

Baldwin, Carl: Adolph Gottlieb. (In "In the Galleries") *Arts* 32:53 D 1957.

_____ Adolph Gottlieb. (In "In the Galleries") *Arts* 32:53 Ja 1958. 1 il.

Berkowitz, M.: Die 7 Biennale von São Paulo. *Kunstwerk* 17:20 N 1963. 1 il.

Berkson, William: Adolph Gottlieb. (In "In the Galleries") *Arts* 40:61 Ap 1966. 1 il.

Bowness, Alan: *The Observer,* London Je 7 1959.

Breuning, Margaret: In Intimate Media. (In "Fifty-Seventh Street in Review") *Arts Digest* 25:22 My 15 1951.

_____ Pictographs by Gottlieb. (In "Fifty-Seventh Street in Review") *Arts Digest* 22:20 N 1 1947.

Burrows, Carlyle: Art: Gottlieb Abstracts Shown. *New York Herald Tribune* Ja 11 1953, p 6.

_____ Art in Review: Mainly in Abstract Form. *New York Herald Tribune* Ja 14 1951.

_____ "Early to Modern." *New York Herald Tribune* Ja 15 1950.

_____ "Gottlieb Abstracts." *New York Herald Tribune* Ap 11 1954.

_____ *New York Herald Tribune* Ja 12 1947.

_____ *New York Herald Tribune* N 9 1947.

_____ Vanguard Work Selected for Exhibition, *New York Herald Tribune* D 30 1951, p 7. 1 il.

Butcher, G. M.: Gottlieb and the New York School. *Art News and Review* 11:9 Je 20 1959.

Butler, Barbara: Movie Stars and Other Members of the Cast. *Art International* 4:2-3:51 1960.

Campbell, Leon: Twenty-Third Corcoran Biennial. *Art News* 52:38 Ap 1953. 1 il.

Chanin, A. L.: The World of Art: Enchantment in the Galleries Reality — and Polished Apples. *The Compass* Ja 14 1951. 1 il.

Coates, Robert M.: The Art Galleries. *The New Yorker* 26: 71 Ja 13 1951.

Crehan, Hubert: Adolph Gottlieb. (In "Reviews and Previews") Art News 59:12 D 1960. 1 il.

Devree, Howard: *New York Times* F 13 1944.

Emmerich, André: The Artist as Collector. *Art in America* 46:25 Summer 1958, por.

Faison, S. Lane, Jr.: Art. *The Nation* 176:38 Ja 10 1953.

Ferling, Lawrence: San Francisco (In "Coast-to-Coast") *Art Digest* 27:13 Mr 15 1953.

Fitzsimmons, James: Adolph Gottlieb. *Everyday Art Quarterly* no. 25:1-4 1953. 3 il, por.

_____ "Art For A Synagogue." *Art Digest* 27:16 Je 1953.

_____ Artists Put Faith in New Ecclesiastic Art. *Art Digest* 26:15, 23 O 15 1951. 2 il.

_____ Gottlieb on Land and Sea. (In "New York") *Art Digest* 27:16 Ja 1 1953. 1 il.

_____ Watercolours, Waterverven, Watercolors. *Art Digest* 27:7 Je 1953.

Fried, Michael: (In "New York Letter") *Art International* 6:75-76 O 25 1962.

Friedman, M.: Private Symbols in Public Statements. *Art News* 62:32-35, 52-53 My 1963. 8 il, cover.

Frigerio, S.: Les expositions à l'étranger. L'exposition internationale de Pittsburgh et les prix d'Institut Carnegie. *Aujourd'hui* 6:62-63 D 1961. 1 il.

Frost, Rosamund: Adolph Gottlieb. (In "The Passing Shows") *Art News* 43:23 F 15 1944.

Geist, Sidney: Platitudes in Stained Glass Attitudes. (In "New York") *Art Digest* 27:17 S 1953.

Genauer, Emily: Abstract Painters' Exhibit. *New York Herald Tribune* Ja 13 1952, p 9.

_____ Art and artists: Church Abstractions. *New York Herald Tribune* O 7 1951.

_____ Arts and Artists: Wall of Glass. *New York Herald Tribune Book Review* S 19 1954, p 16. 1 il.

_____ *New York Herald Tribune,* Ja 10 1960.

_____ *New York Herald Tribune Book Review* F 3 1957.

_____ *New York Herald Tribune Book Review,* Ja 12 1958.

_____ *New York Herald Tribune Book Review,* Ja 11 1959.

_____ *New York World Telegram* D 15 1945.

_____ A Variety of Painter-Poets: New Gottlieb Abstracts. *New York Herald Tribune Book Review* F 3 1957.

_____ The Young in Art. *New York Herald Tribune Book Review* Ap 25 1954. 1 il.

Goldwater, Robert: Reflections on the New York School. *Quadrum* no. 8:17-36 1960. 1 il.

Goossen, E. C.: Adolph Gottlieb. *Monterey Peninsula Herald* My 12 1954.

_____ *Monterey Peninsula Herald* D 18 1957.

Gordon, A.: San Paulo Biennale. *Connoiseur* 155: 55 Ja 1964. 1 il.

Greenberg, Clement: After Abstract Expressionism. *Art International* 6:24-32 O 25 1962. 1 il.

_____ American Type Painting. *Partisan Review* 22:2:185-186 Spring 1955.

———— Art. *The Nation* 165:629 D 6 1947.

———— Art. *The Nation* 168:221 F 19 1949.

Grosser: *The Nation* 188:78 Ja 24 1959.

Hess, Thomas B.: Abstract Art in America. *Paris Review* 1954.

———— Adolph Gottlieb. (In "Reviews and Previews") *Art News* 47:49, 58 F 1949. 1 il.

———— Adolph Gottlieb. (In "Fifty-Seventh Street in Review") *Art Digest* 25:21 Ja 15 1951. 1 il.

———— Adolph Gottlieb. (In "Reviews and Previews") *Art News* 49:47 Ja 1951. 1 il.

———— The New York Salon. *Arts Digest* 28:25, 56 F 1954. 1 il.

Hinrichsen, A. D.: Beauty at the Biennale No. 7 at São Paulo. *Studio* 166:256 D 1963. 1 il.

Hunter, Sam: Guggenheim Sampler. *Art Digest* 28:9,31 My 15 1954. 1 il.

———— *New York Times* N 9 1947.

———— *New York Times* Je 30 1949.

Huxtable, Ada Louise: Gottlieb's Glass Wall. *Arts Digest* 29:9 Ja 15 1955. 2 il.

*The Intrasubjectives,* preface by Samuel Kootz, Kootz Gallery, S 14-0 3 1949.

Jewell, Edward Alden: *New York Times* F 27 1944.

———— *New York Times* Mr 18 1945.

Judd, Donald: Adolph Gottlieb. (In "In the Galleries") *Arts* 35:52-53 D 1960.

Kees, Weldon: *The Nation* 170:20 Ja 7 1950.

Kimball: *Berkshire Eagle,* Williamstown My 12 1954.

Kozloff, Max: The Critical Reception of Abstract-Expressionism. *Arts* 40:27-33 D 1965. 1 il.

Krasne, Belle: Adolph Gottlieb. (In "Fifty-Seventh Street in Review") *Art Digest* 25:21 Ja 15 1951. 1 il.

———— Gottlieb Through the Magnifying Glass. *Art Digest* 24:16 Ja 15 1952. 1 il.

———— No More Prison Bars. (In "New York") *Art Digest* 26:15 Ja 15 1952. 1 il.

Krauss, Rosalind: (In "New York") *Art Forum* 4:49 My 1966. 1 il.

Kruse: *Brooklyn Eagle* F 13 1944.

La Farge, Henry A.: Ecclesiastical art. *Art News* 52:50 Summer 1953.

Langsner, Jules: Cremean, Gottlieb, Irwin (In "Art news from Los Angeles") *Art News* 58:60 Summer 1959.

———— More about the School of New York. *Arts and Architecture* 68:20 My 1951.

Laws: *Manchester Guardian* Je 16 1959.

Lippard, Lucy R.: New York Letter: Off Color. *Art International* 10:76-77 Ap 1966. 1 il.

Lonngren, Lillian: Abstract Expressionism in the American Scene. *Art International* 2:54-56 1958. 11 il.

Louchheim, Aline B.: ABC (or XYZ) of Abstract Art. The *New York Times Magazine* Jl 11 1948, p 16-17, 42-43. 1 il.

———— Architect, Painter — And the Mural, *New York Times* O 1 1950.

———— Art for Religion. *New York Times* My 24 1953, p 8. 1 il.

———— Modern Decoration for a Synagogue. *New York Times* O 7 1951.

———— Two Shows with Unusual Themes: Art for a Temple. *New York Times* O 7 1951.

Loveman: Part of inner men. *Newsweek* 26:86 D 31 1945. il.

Lowe, Jeanette: Gottlieb's Dream-Like Semi-Abstractions. (In "Exhibitions of the Week") *Art News* 38:20-21 Ap 27 1940. 1 il.

McBride, Henry: *New York Sun* N 7 1947.

Mellquist, Jerome: Adolph Gottlieb. (In "In the Galleries") *Arts* 31:53 F 1957. 1 il.

Michelson, Annette: Gottlieb (and Clement Greenberg) at The Rive Droite. (In "Paris") *Arts* 33:18 Je 1959. 1 il.

———— *New York Herald Tribune,* Paris, Ap 8 1959.

Mocsanyi, Paul: Art in Review. *United Press Red Letter* Ja 25-26 1950.

———— *United Press Red Letter* My 14-15 1954, p 77.

Motherwell, Robert: *Seventeen Modern American Painters,* Beverly Hills, Frank Perls Gallery, Ja 11-F 7 1951.

Newman, Barnett B.: La pintura de Tamayo y Gottlieb. *l a Revista Delga* 2:16-25 Ap 1945. 5 il. Text in Spanish.

Nordland, Gerald: *Frontier* 11:20 My 1959.

O'Doherty, Brian: Adolph Gottlieb: The dualism of an inner life. *New York Times* F 23 1964.

———— *New York Times* O 5 1962.

O'Hara, Frank: Adolph Gottlieb's. (In "Reviews and Previews") *Art News* 53:47 Ap 1954. 1 il.

Piene, Nan R.: Marlborough-Gerson. (In "New York: Gallery Notes") *Art in America* 54:121 Ja 1966. 1 il.

Porter, Fairfield: Adolph Gottlieb. (In "Reviews and Previews") *Art News* 50:40-41 Ja 1952. 1 il.

———— Adolph Gottlieb. (In "Reviews and Previews") *Art News* 51:44 Ja 1953.

Portner, Leslie Judd: A Challenge to Spectators (In "Art in Washington") *Washington Post* Mr 30 1952. 1 il.

Preston, Stuart: About Art and Artists. *New York Times* Ap 7 1954.

———— Among The Early Shows. *New York Times* S 17 1950.

———— Among Current Shows. *New York Times* Ap 11 1954.

———— Chiefly Abstract. *New York Times* Ja 11 1953, p 11.

———— New Year Openings. *New York Times* Ja 7 1951.

———— *New York Times* F 2 1957.

———— *New York Times* Ja 11 1959.

_____ _New York Times_ N 13 1960.

_____ Recent Openings. _New York Times_ Ja 15 1950.

_____ Recent Openings. _New York Times_ Ja 13 1952, p 9.

Read, Sir Herbert and Arnason, H. Harvard: Dialogue on modern U. S. painting. _Art News_ 59: 32-36 My 1960. 1 il.

Reed, Judith Kaye: Gottlieb Pictographs. (In "Fifty-Seventh Street in Review") _Art Digest_ 23:20 F 1 1949.

_____ Modern Pictographs. _Art Digest_ 21:19 Ja 1 1947. 1 il.

_____ New Artists Honored, Abstraction Crowned at Whitney Annual. _Art Digest_ 24:7 Ja 1 1950.

Rexroth, Kenneth: Americans seen abroad. (In "U. S. art across time and space") _Art News_ 58:30-33, 52, 54. Summer 1959. 1 il.

Riley, Maude Kemper: Gottlieb's Enigmas. _Art Digest_ 19:49 Ap 1 1945. 1 il.

_____ Adolph Gottlieb. (In "New York Exhibitions") _MKR's art outlook_ 1:28:2 Ja 20 1947. 1 il.

Robinson, Amy: Adolph Gottlieb's. (In "Reviews and Previews") _Art News_ 48:47 Ja 1950. 1 il.

Rosenberg, Harold: _Introduction á la Peinture Modern Américaine,_ Paris, Galerie Maeght, Mr-Ap 1947.

Rosenblum, Robert: Adolph Gottlieb: New Murals. _Art Digest_ 28:11 Ap 15 1954. 1 il.

Rosenstein, Harris: Adolph Gottlieb. (In "In the Galleries") _Arts_ 40:61 Ap 1966. 1 il.

_____ Adolph Gottlieb. (In "Reviews and Previews") _Art News_ 64:16 F 1966. 1 il.

_____ Gottlieb at the Summit. _Art News_ 65:42-43 Ap 1966. 3 il.

Rubin, William: Adolph Gottlieb. _Art International_ 3:3-4:34-37 1959. 6 il.

_____ "The New York School" — Then and Now. Part II. _Art International_ 2:4-5:19-22 My-Je 1958.

Rudikoff, Sonya: Space in Abstract Painting. _Partisan Review_ 25:297-304 Spring 1958.

_____ Tangible Abstract Art. _Partisan Review_ 24: 275-281 Spring 1957.

Sandler, Irving H.: Adolph Gottlieb. _Art News_ 57:10 F 1959. 1 il.

_____ Adolph Gottlieb. (In "Reviews and Previews") _Art News_ 58:14 F 1960.

_____ (In "New York Letter") _Quadrum_ no 14:123-124 1963. 1 il.

_____ A Selection of One-Man Shows. (In "New York Letter"). _Art International_ 4:26-27 D 31 1960. 2 il, cover.

Sawin, Martica: Adolph Gottlieb. (In "In the Galleries") _Arts_ 33:54-55 F 1959. 1 il.

_____ (In "New York Letter") _Art International_ 3 1-2:46 1959.

Sawyer, Kenneth: Painting and Sculpture: The New York Season. _Craft Horizons_ 22:52-55, 70 My-Je 1962.

Schwartz, Marvin D.: Adolph Gottlieb. (In "News and Views from New York") _Apollo_ 67:63 F 1958.

Seckler, Dorothy Gees: Adolph Gottlieb makes a facade. _Art News_ 54:42-45, 61-62 Mr 1955, 15 il.

_____ Artist in America: Victim of the Culture Boom? _Art in America_ 51:34-35 D 1963. por.

Sorzano, Margo: 17 Modern American Painters. _Arts and Architecture_ 68:26-28 Ja 1951. 1 il.

Stroup, Jon: "Time Out." _Town and Country_ Mr 1945, p 86.

Swenson, G. R.: Adolph Gottlieb. (In "Reviews and previews") _Art News_ 61:10 N 1962. 1 il.

Tillim, Sidney: Adolph Gottlieb. (In "New York Exhibitions: In the Galleries") _Arts_ 38:32 Ap 1964.

_____ Month in Review. (In "New York Exhibitions") _Arts_ 37:38-39 N 1962. 2 il.

Tyler, Parker: Adolph Gottlieb. _Art News_ 55:8 F 1957.

_____ Adolph Gottlieb. (In "Reviews and previews") _Art News_ 56:10 D 1957. 1 il.

_____ Adolph Gottlieb. (In "Reviews and previews") _Art News_ 56:17 Ja 1958.

Valente, Alfredo: Adolph Gottlieb. _Promenade_ F 1949, p 40. 1 il., por.

Ventura, Anita: Adolph Gottlieb. (In "In the Galleries") _Arts_ 34:62 F 1960.

Wolf, Ben: Blended Moderns. _Art Digest_ 20:10 D 15 1945.

Wolfson, Victor: Woman Terror (In _Women: A collaboration of artists and writers_ by Samuel M. Kootz, Samuel M. Kootz Editions, c. 1948 p 29-31. il.